· STRATEGIES · FOR · SUCCESS ·

New York

Grade 8
Intermediate-Level
Science Test

A REVIEW BOOK

Globe Fearon

Upper Saddle River, New Jersey
www.globefearon.com

Reviewers

We would like to thank the following educators, who provided valuable comments and suggestions during the development of this book:

Larry Beck, Isaac E. Young Middle School, New Rochelle, New York

M. Blanche Hogquist, JHS 117, Bronx, New York

Molly Lane, Rush-Henrietta Central School District, Henrietta, New York

Claudia Toback, New York State Earth Science Mentor, New York City Mentor STANYS Middle Level SAR

Martha Kelly, Belleville Middle School, Belleville, New Jersey

Educational Consultants

Michael DuPré and Joyce Valenti, SEEDS for Learning, Farmington, New York

Project Staff

Executive Editor: Jane Petlinski

Supervising Editor: Stephanie Petron Cahill

Lead Editor: Maury Solomon

Production Editor: Laura Benford-Sullivan

Designer: Jennifer Visco

Market Manager: Douglas Falk

Editorial, Design, and Production Services: Mazer Corporation

Manufacturing Supervisor: Mark Cirillo

ISBN: 0-130-23753-1

Printed in the United States of America

5 6 7 8 9 10   04 03 02 01

1-800-848-9500
www.globefearon.com

CONTENTS

CONTENTS

To the Student

The purpose of this review book is to help prepare you for the New York Grade 8 Intermediate-Level Science Test. The questions on the test cover the basic content of the science you have learned from Grades 5 through 8. In addition, the test assesses your ability to plot graphs from data, fill in data tables, design experiments, do math, write short-answer responses, and demonstrate a number of other skills. These are skills you have already learned in your classes. This review book will help you to practice those skills so that you can do your best on the test.

The New York Grade 8 Intermediate-Level Science Test has four parts. Part A contains multiple-choice questions. It tests your understanding of the basic concepts you have learned in your science classes. As a way of helping you to recall that material, this book provides a review chapter outlining the main concepts you have learned and a chapter on answering multiple-choice questions. In addition, many test-like questions and content clues related to that science content are provided throughout the book. As you work with the content and skills reviewed in this book, you will recall what you have learned already, and you will learn ways to apply that knowledge to a testing situation.

Part B of the New York Grade 8 Intermediate-Level Science Test contains multiple-choice and short-answer questions. In Part B, you will be asked to interpret charts, graphs, diagrams, and other visuals. This review book includes an entire chapter on how to interpret diagrams and additional chapters on how to read charts and graphs and analyze data. Many of the other chapters also contain practices that include questions on visuals.

Part C of the New York Grade 8 Intermediate-Level Science Test will ask you to apply your knowledge and skills to real-world situations. You will be asked to form hypotheses, make predictions, and use other science inquiry skills in your answers. This review book will help you to accomplish those tasks by providing a chapter on science inquiry skills. The situations presented in that chapter are all taken from real life.

Part D of the New York Grade 8 Intermediate-Level Science Test is a laboratory performance test. In Part D, you will go to an area where three experiments have been set up for you. You will be given step-by-step instructions telling you what to do. Part of the instructions will include questions that you will answer as you do the experiment. Each experiment will take between ten and fifteen minutes. This review book outlines the techniques you will need to be successful on Part D of the test. You will review measuring, how to use a microscope and other lab equipment, and lab safety procedures. Then you will be given the setups for a variety of lab experiments as practice.

The best way to succeed on any test is to go into it prepared. The strategies and practices found in this book will help you to prepare. If you use the opportunities this book provides and get proper rest the night before the test, you should feel confident and ready for the test. Good luck!

CHAPTER 1

Reviewing the Content

To be successful on the Grade 8 Intermediate-Level Science Test, you will need to recall and understand many different scientific concepts. Although you don't need to know every detail about a subject, you do need to have a general understanding of the content you have been learning in your science classes over the last several years.

This chapter will help you identify areas you need to review. It will provide you with a chance to revisit the scientific concepts you learned earlier. Your self-confidence should increase as you add to what you already know and understand about science.

Using This Chapter

This chapter is organized around 12 "key ideas." For each key idea, you will find a summary statement and a vocabulary list. The vocabulary list contains words found in the Glossary at the end of this book. Each key idea is followed by important points or concepts. You will need to understand all of the concepts presented to master a key idea.

As you read each concept, decide whether or not you completely understand it. Be sure you understand each vocabulary word (in **bold** print) and can define it and use it in a sentence. Put a check mark (✓) in the box at the beginning of a concept if you understand everything contained in that concept. If you don't fully understand a concept, leave the box blank.

For example, here is a concept from The Living Environment, Key Idea 1:

❑ The **cell membrane** surrounds the cell and controls the movement of substances into and out of the cell.

As you read that concept, ask yourself these questions:

- Do I know what a cell membrane is?
- Do I know where the membrane is in relation to the other cell parts?
- Do I understand the function of the cell membrane?

If you answer "yes" to all of those questions, place a check mark in the box. Leave the box blank if you don't understand the concept. Remember that this chapter will help you identify what you know and what you need to learn more about.

After completing the two pages for each key idea, write down in a separate notebook any concepts that you did not check off. These are the concepts that you will need to review.

Finding Out More

After you identify the concepts you need to review, you may need to find out more information about those concepts. Here are some places to look for information and people to ask for help:

- encyclopedias
- books at your local or school library
- educational Web sites
- science teachers or teacher's aides
- peer tutoring groups

In addition, the other chapters in this book contain information about some of the most important scientific concepts. As you work through the chapters, pay careful attention to important science facts that you need to recall to be successful on the Grade 8 Intermediate-Level Science Test.

Living and Nonliving Things

The Living Environment: Key Idea 1

> Living things are both similar to and different from each other and from nonliving things.

Vocabulary Terms cell, cell membrane, cellular respiration, cell wall, chloroplast, chlorophyll, circulatory system, classification, cytoplasm, digestive system, excretory system, gland, disease, endocrine system, hormone, immune system, kingdom, microscope, mitochondria, muscular system, nervous system, nucleus, organ, organelle, organism, respiratory system, skeletal system, species, system, tissue

Put a check (✓) next to the concepts that you know.

The Basic Units of Life Living things, called **organisms**, are made up of **cells.** Cells are the basic units of life. Some organisms have only one cell. Others have millions of cells. All cells, whether they form simple or complex organisms, have certain things in common.

❑ Most cells are so small that they must be viewed using a **microscope.**

❑ The **cell membrane** surrounds the cell and controls the movement of substances into and out of the cell.

❑ Near the center of the cell is the **nucleus.** The nucleus controls the other parts of the cell and the cell's activities.

❑ The cell is filled mostly with a watery substance called **cytoplasm.** Small structures in the cytoplasm, called **organelles,** carry out different jobs for the cell.

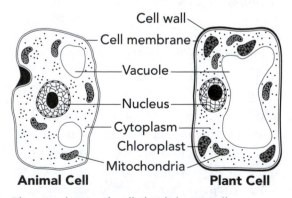

Animal Cell   **Plant Cell**

*Plant and animal cells both have cell membranes to protect them. However, plant cells also have **cell walls** for extra support.*

❑ Cells contain **mitochondria.** These organelles use the gas oxygen to release energy from food molecules. The process cells use to release energy from food molecules is called **cellular respiration.**

❑ Plant cells have **chloroplasts.** These organelles contain the green material **chlorophyll,** which traps light energy from the Sun. Inside chloroplasts, water and carbon dioxide use the energy from the Sun to make food.

From Cells to Systems Plants and animals have groups of specialized cells that do different jobs.

❑ Groups of cells that work together to perform a special function are called **tissues.** Your blood is a tissue made up of several types of cells that aid in the exchange of gases.

❑ Tissues that work together to do a specific job are called **organs.** Your heart is an organ. A group of organs that work together form a **system.** Several systems can interact with each other.

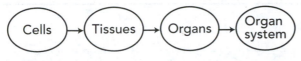

Plants and animals are made up of complex body systems built from specialized cells.

Human Body Systems Human body systems work together to provide energy, remove wastes, and carry out other life functions.

❑ The **circulatory system** brings needed oxygen to cells and removes wastes from cells. The circulatory system includes the heart, blood, and blood vessels.

❑ The **skeletal system** is made up of bone and cartilage. This system supports and protects the body. It also works with the **muscular system** to allow movement.

❑ The **digestive system** is responsible for the mechanical and chemical breakdown of food into food molecules. The food molecules are then transported to cells and used by them for energy.

❑ The **respiratory system** consists mainly of the lungs. It also includes the tubes and passageways through which air moves.

❑ The **nervous** and **endocrine systems** together control the body's responses to changes in the environment. They also regulate growth, development, and reproduction.

❑ **Hormones** are chemicals released by organs called **glands**. Many glands are part of the endocrine system. Hormones affect the way other parts of the body work.

❑ The **excretory system** disposes of body wastes in the form of liquids. It also eliminates excess body heat.

❑ The breakdown in the structures or functions of an organism can cause **disease**. Protecting the body from disease is the work of the **immune system**.

Classifying Organisms Biologists group organisms by their characteristics, structures, and origins. This is called **classification**. Biologists study organisms to determine how they should be grouped.

❑ There are five main groups in biological classification. Each one of these main groups is called a **kingdom**.

Kingdom	Examples
1. Moneran	Bacteria Blue-green bacteria
2. Protist	Protozoa Algae
3. Fungus	Molds Yeasts Mushrooms
4. Plant	Seed plants Cone-bearing plants Ferns
5. Animal	Insects Fish Reptiles Birds Mammals

Organisms are placed into a kingdom and then broken down into smaller and smaller groups. The smallest classification group is a ***species.***

❑ Some scientists think there should be a sixth kingdom, made up of some organisms now classified as bacteria.

 In your notebook, list the concepts that you need to review. Then write down sources you can use to learn more about these concepts.

Genetic Information

The Living Environment: Key Idea 2

An organism's cells contain DNA, which acts as a set of instructions that determine the organism's traits. This set of instructions is passed from one generation to the next during reproduction.

Vocabulary Terms asexual reproduction, chromosome, DNA, dominant trait, egg, fertilization, gene, genetic engineering, heredity, meiosis, mitosis, offspring, pedigree chart, Punnett square, recessive trait, sexual reproduction, sperm, trait, zygote

Put a check (✓) next to the concepts that you know.

Asexual Reproduction The production of **offspring** from only one parent is called **asexual reproduction**. Offspring are the new organisms created by living things.

❑ The division of a cell's nucleus that results in two identical "daughter" cells is called **mitosis.**

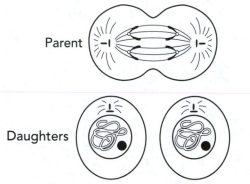

During mitosis the nucleus of a cell makes an exact copy of itself.

❑ Some single-celled organisms, such as bacteria, reproduce mainly through a process called binary fission, which uses mitosis. Offspring produced by binary fission are identical to the parent. In multicellular organisms, mitosis is used to replace old cells.

Sexual Reproduction The production of offspring from two parents is called **sexual reproduction**. Offspring usually show some of the characteristics, or **traits,** of each parent.

❑ The type of cell division that results in reproductive cells, or sex cells, is called **meiosis.** Each reproductive cell has half the number of **chromosomes,** or genetic material, as the parent cell.

❑ The female parent produces a reproductive cell called an **egg.** The male parent produces a reproductive cell called a **sperm.**

❑ When an egg and a sperm join, a new cell, called a **zygote,** is formed. The zygote has the same number of chromosomes as each parent. Half came from the father, half came from the mother.

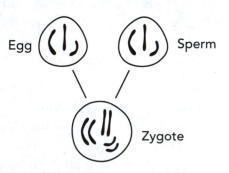

The joining of the egg and sperm cells to form a zygote is called **fertilization.**

Heredity Traits are passed by **genes** from the parent or parents to the next generation. The passing of genes from parents to offspring is called **heredity.**

❑ Hereditary information is found in the body's genes. Genes are units of **DNA,** a chemical found in the nucleus of every cell in an organism's body. A human cell contains many thousands of different genes.

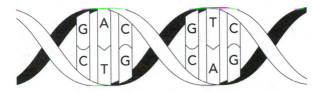

DNA is found on chromosomes in the nuclei of cells and in the cytoplasm of monerans. It codes and stores genetic information. Its function is to direct the cell on how to carry out life processes.

❑ When a zygote is formed during fertilization, the chromosomes from the egg and sperm are organized into pairs.

❑ A single trait, or characteristic, of an organism can be determined by one pair or by many pairs of genes found on the chromosomes. Some examples of hereditary traits in humans are hair and eye color, height, intelligence, sense of humor, and musical abilities.

❑ Gregor Mendel was the first to describe how traits are passed on from generation to generation in all organisms.

❑ Some traits are dominant and some are recessive. Traits can also be inherited in a few other ways.

❑ In an organism a **dominant trait** is one that will show its effect no matter the effect of its partner trait.

❑ A **recessive trait** is one that will be masked by the dominant partner trait. Recessive traits are not lost. They may show up in later generations.

❑ The probability of a trait being expressed, or seen in an organism, can be predicted using models. Two models are **pedigree charts** and **Punnett squares.**

❑ A Punnett square shows the probability of an offspring showing a specific trait. In the cross below, the probability of offspring having green pods is 3 out of 4, or 75 percent. The probability of offspring having yellow pods is 1 out of 4, or 25 percent.

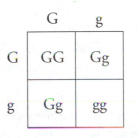

	G	g
G	GG	Gg
g	Gg	gg

G = Dominant gene (green pods)
g = Recessive gene (yellow pods)

❑ Controlled breeding by humans has been used to produce organisms, usually plants, with desired traits.

❑ **Genetic engineering** is a set of methods used by scientists to alter an organism's DNA.

In your notebook, list the concepts that you need to review. Then write down sources you can use to learn more about these concepts.

Change Over Time

The Living Environment: Key Idea 3

Individual organisms and species are constantly changing, evolving, and adapting to their environments. This has led to the great diversity among species existing today.

Vocabulary Terms
adaptation, competition, diversity, endangered, environment, evolution, extinct, extinction, fossil, mutation, natural selection, resource, sedimentary rock, variation

Put a check (✓) next to the concepts that you know.

Diversity Among Organisms Every organism has unique characteristics called **adaptations**, or adaptive traits, that help it compete for **resources** that must be shared. Examples of such resources are food and territory. If an organism competes successfully, it will likely survive and reproduce.

❏ Most **environments** have a limited supply of resources. Environment is everything that surrounds an organism. There is **competition** for these resources.

❏ Differences among the members of a species are called **variation.** Variation provides **diversity,** or a wide range of traits, within a species. It helps organisms adapt to changes in their environment.

❏ Variation may give some members of a species an advantage in competition. It may make them more likely to survive. The advantages may then be passed on to their offspring.

❏ The ways in which variations in organisms occur determine how well these organisms will compete in their environment for resources. It also helps determine the organism's survival.

❏ Most adaptive characteristics are inherited behaviors or traits. Parents pass these on to their offspring through sexual reproduction.

❏ Parents also pass on learned behaviors. They teach their offspring what they have learned. These learned behaviors allow individual offspring to adapt better to their environment.

❏ Natural events, such as flood, fire, or drought, can change the environment. They destroy living space and resources. When these events occur, organisms living in that environment that have beneficial adaptive traits due to variation may survive. Others must move to a new place. If they don't, they will die.

❏ Offspring whose variations allow them to adapt to a changing environment are more likely to survive and reproduce. This is part of the **natural selection** theory developed by Charles Darwin.

❏ Species in danger of dying out are said to be **endangered**. When there are no more living organisms in a species, the species is said to be **extinct. Extinction** of species is very common over geologic time.

❏ Humans have adapted successfully to many different environments. Huge increases in the human population have caused many wildlife areas to disappear. This has led in recent years to a decline in the numbers of many species.

Mutation A sudden, permanent change in an organism's genetic material, or DNA, is called a **mutation**. Mutations lead to greater variations within populations of organisms.

❑ Some mutations are harmful. If a mutation is harmful, the organism may be less able to survive in its environment. If the organism dies before it can reproduce, the mutation will not be passed on.

❑ Some mutations are helpful. They allow the individual to adapt better to its environment. If this individual survives and reproduces, the mutation may be passed on to its offspring.

Evidence of Evolution Both individual organisms and whole species change over time. This is the theory of **evolution**. There is much **fossil** evidence to support this theory.

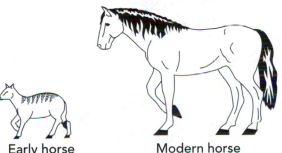

Early horse   Modern horse

Fossil evidence shows that the modern horse evolved from a much smaller animal.

❑ Fossils are the remains of organisms that died long ago. Fossils show that a great variety of species existed in the past. Many have become extinct, due to sudden changes in the environment. Fossils also show that many types of organisms have changed greatly over time.

❑ **Sedimentary rocks** tell us a lot about the history of the Earth. As layers of this rock form from sediments that are laid down and compressed, they bury the remains of organisms.

❑ Fossils of different organisms are found in different layers of sedimentary rock. The layer in which a fossil is found in rock may indicate its age. It may also give clues to the environment in which the organism lived.

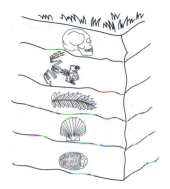

In rock layers that have not been disturbed, older rock lies below younger rock. So fossils found in these lower layers are older than those found in the upper layers.

❑ Small changes in offspring can accumulate over many generations. This leads to descendants that are very different from their ancestors.

❑ Fossils often show us that the ancestors of most modern species had simpler structures than those of their descendants.

❑ Evolution and natural selection can sometimes be seen in action. Due to their short life span, some species of insects and bacteria have changed greatly through environmental pressures in just a few years.

In your notebook, list the concepts that you need to review. Then write down sources you can use to learn more about these concepts.

Reproduction and Development

The Living Environment: Key Idea 4

Organisms must reproduce if a species is to continue. Many organisms need only one parent for reproduction to take place. Others need two parents. Some can have one or two parents.

Vocabulary Terms budding, embryo, life cycle, metamorphosis, pistil, pollination, spore, stamen

Put a check (✓) next to the concepts you know.

Reproduction with One Parent Some organisms reproduce asexually, using only one parent. There are several types of asexual reproduction.

❑ Some simple organisms reproduce using binary fission, which involves mitosis. Binary fission is the division of a one-celled organism into two identical daughter cells.

❑ Another kind of asexual reproduction, called **budding,** is used by organisms such as yeast.

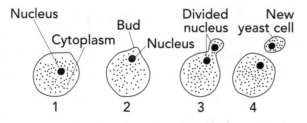

In budding, a new cell is formed from a tiny bud on the parent cell.

❑ Molds reproduce asexually using reproductive cells called **spores.** When a spore case grows to full size, it bursts open. It sends spores flying through the air. Some spores land on a food source such as bread. If the temperature and moisture levels are right, the spores develop into new mature molds.

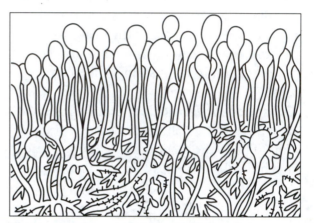

This is what bread mold looks like under a microscope.

❑ In multicellular organisms, mitosis is responsible for the growth, health, and repair of existing body cells.

Reproduction with Two Parents
Methods of sexual reproduction vary. However, all types involve the combining of reproductive cells to begin the development of a new individual.

❑ In many organisms, including plants and animals, the female parent produces eggs. The male parent produces sperm (pollen in plants).

❑ The sperm and the egg each carry half of the genetic information for the new individual. When an egg is fertilized by a sperm, a zygote is formed.

- Fertilization in some animal species takes place outside the body. This is called *external fertilization.* Salmon and frogs are two animals that use external fertilization.

- Fertilization in some animal species takes place inside the body. This is called *internal fertilization.* Birds, snakes, and dogs are some animals that use internal fertilization.

- Fertilization results in a zygote, which is made up of one cell. Soon after it forms, the zygote divides and becomes two cells. Each of these cells then divide. Cell division continues, and a young organism, or **embryo,** forms.

- Each body cell in a multicellular organism has the same exact genetic information.

- In its first three months, a human embryo develops tissues and some organs. By six months, all the organs are formed, and many body features are developed. By nine months, the organs and features have developed enough to allow the baby to live safely outside the mother.

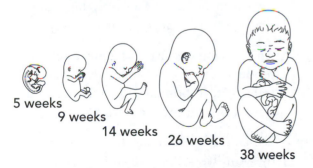

5 weeks
9 weeks
14 weeks
26 weeks
38 weeks

The human embryo develops in the uterus for about 38 weeks, or nine months.

- Body structures and functions change as organisms age.

Plant Reproduction
In many plants flowers are the organs of reproduction.

- Flowers contain reproductive parts called **pistils** and **stamens.** The pistil is the female reproductive organ, and the stamen is the male reproductive organ.

- **Pollination** leads to the fertilizing in flowers of a female cell by the male cell. Its final result is a zygote that develops into a seed. The seed contains the young plant and food to help the young plant grow.

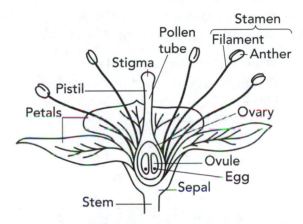

Stamen
Pollen tube
Filament
Anther
Stigma
Pistil
Petals
Ovary
Ovule
Egg
Sepal
Stem

During pollination, grains of pollen land on the plant part known as the stigma. Sperm cells from the pollen grain move through a pollen tube into the plant's ovary. There, the sperm fertilizes the egg.

Life Cycles
Different organisms have different patterns of growth and development. These are called **life cycles.**

- In some species, such as humans, the young resemble the adult. In other species, such as many insects and amphibians, the young go through a series of extreme physical changes in the body. This cycle is called **metamorphosis.**

In your notebook, list the concepts that you need to review. Then write down sources you can use to learn more about these concepts.

Meeting Daily Needs

The Living Environment: Key Idea 5

Organisms must be able to get and use resources, to grow, to reproduce, and to adapt to a constantly changing environment.

Vocabulary Terms Calorie, carbohydrate, carnivore, consumer, decomposer, digestion, energy, excretion, fat, glucose, herbivore, homeostasis, metabolism, mineral, nutrient, omnivore, photosynthesis, producer, protein, respiration, stimulus and response, transport, vitamin

Put a check (✓) next to the concepts that you know.

Food and Energy All organisms need **energy** to stay alive and carry out life processes. They get this energy from food.

❑ Plants make their own food during a chemical reaction called **photosynthesis**. Photosynthesis takes place in the leaf. Water and carbon dioxide are combined in the presence of sunlight to produce glucose. Oxygen is given off as a byproduct of this reaction.

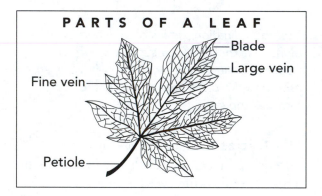

PARTS OF A LEAF

Blade — Large vein — Fine vein — Petiole

Veins in a leaf make up the leaf's transport system.

❑ Animals cannot make their own food. Instead, they must obtain food from their environment.

❑ Animals and plants have many different body plans and structures. An organism's body plan helps determine how it will carry out the processes of **digestion** and **respiration**.

❑ Digestion is the breaking down of food into a form that can be used by an organism. The bodies of plants and animals make chemicals that change food into a usable form.

❑ Plants and animals use **glucose**, a simple sugar, as fuel. Oxygen is used to help release the energy in food or to break the bonds that hold food molecules together.

❑ Once food is digested, **nutrients** must be carried to all parts of a living thing, and waste products must be carried away.

❑ The moving of nutrients and waste products throughout the body is called **transport**. In humans, the nutrients and waste travel in the bloodstream.

❑ Oxygen is found in air. It is a gas needed by most living things.

❑ Respiration is the internal and external process that provides oxygen to the body's cells and removes waste gases. Cellular respiration is the internal chemical process that cells use to release energy from food molecules.

❑ The waste products of cellular respiration are carbon dioxide and water. **Excretion** is the process of removing these and other waste materials from the body.

Sharing the Environment All organisms in an environment compete for the resources necessary for life. All organisms need food, water, air, warmth, and living space.

❑ The survival of an organism depends on its ability to sense and respond to its internal and external environment. This is called **stimulus and response.**

❑ **Homeostasis** is the ability of an organism to keep conditions inside its body constant, whatever the outside conditions.

❑ Toxic substances, or poisons, infectious diseases, and other outside influences may disrupt health, growth, and the homeostasis of one's body.

Feeding Relationships The methods of getting nutrients vary among organisms.

❑ Food provides organisms with energy. The energy in food is measured in **Calories.**

❑ Organisms that make their own food are called **producers.** Producers include plants, some protists, and many bacteria.

❑ **Consumers** are animals, some bacteria, and fungi that must obtain their food from the environment.

❑ Animals that obtain energy by eating only plants are called **herbivores.** Animals that eat both plants and other animals are called **omnivores.** Animals that eat only other animals are called **carnivores.**

❑ Organisms that decompose wastes or consume dead organisms are called **decomposers.**

Diet and Nutrition The foods you eat contain a variety of nutrients, including **carbohydrates, fats, vitamins, proteins, minerals,** and water.

❑ A proper diet provides the energy for growth, health, and metabolic processes. **Metabolism** refers to all the chemical reactions in the organism's body. Metabolism is influenced by hormones, exercise, and diet.

❑ The number of Calories a person needs each day is based on size, age, sex, and activity level. An imbalance of nutrients can result in weight gain, weight loss, or disease.

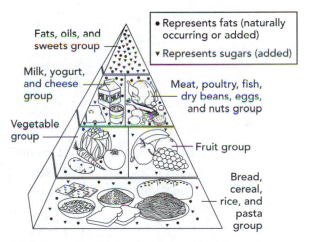

The Food Guide Pyramid was developed to help people choose a healthful, balanced diet. The nutrients people need the greatest amounts of are at the base.

❑ Certain amounts of vitamins and minerals are needed by your body to develop properly. Not getting enough of these nutrients can cause disease.

In your notebook, list the concepts that you need to review. Then write down sources you can use to learn more about these concepts.

Energy in Ecosystems

The Living Environment: Key Idea 6

All organisms depend on living and nonliving parts of the environment for survival. Energy and matter flow from one organism to another. Matter is recycled.

Vocabulary Terms consumer, ecosystem, energy pyramid, food chain, food web, primary consumer, predator, prey, secondary consumer, tertiary consumer

Put a check (✓) next to the concepts that you know.

The Role of Producers Plants and some other organisms are producers. They make their own food.

❑ On land the main producers are plants. In lakes and oceans, the main producers are algae, protists, and plankton.

❑ Sunlight is the main source of energy in most **ecosystems.** An ecosystem is a community of living things and all the nonliving things with which the community interacts.

❑ Most of the energy that enters the environment as sunlight is eventually lost as heat.

❑ Photosynthesis is the process green plants use to make food from sunlight. The energy from the sunlight is converted by the process into chemical energy. It is then stored in the plant's cells as a simple sugar.

❑ The oxygen released by photosynthesis provides most of the oxygen in the air.

❑ Food provides fuel and building materials for all organisms. All living organisms, including plants, must release energy from food to carry out life processes.

The Role of Consumers Energy stored in food passes from one organism to another. A model of these interactions is a **food chain.**

❑ Most food chains start with the Sun, which provides producers such as plants with the energy they need to make food. Most organisms directly or indirectly use the food made by plants to get energy.

❑ **Consumers** get energy by eating other organisms in the food chain. All consumers, directly or indirectly, use food made by producers to meet their energy needs.

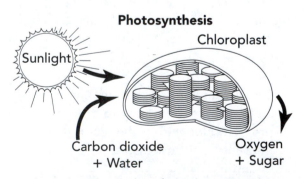

Photosynthesis

Carbon dioxide is taken from the atmosphere and oxygen is released during photosynthesis.

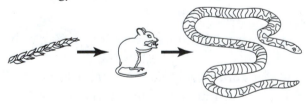

The arrows in a food chain show the direction of the energy flow.

- An organism that eats only plants, such as a rabbit, is called a **primary consumer**. Primary consumers are also known as herbivores.

- Consumers that eat primary consumers are **secondary consumers**. A weasel that eats rabbits is a secondary consumer.

- **Tertiary consumers** are consumers that eat secondary consumers. A hawk that eats a weasel is a tertiary consumer. Depending on what they prefer to eat, people can be primary, secondary, or tertiary consumers.

- Decomposers feed on the wastes or bodies of dead organisms. The nutrients left in what the decomposer does not eat are returned to the soil.

- An **energy pyramid** shows how energy is lost through a food chain. The producers at the bottom of the pyramid have the most energy. Animals gain only a small amount of energy from the food they eat.

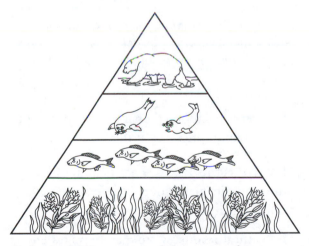

Only about 10 percent of the energy from one level is passed on to the next level in an energy pyramid.

Food Webs Food chains that are linked together in an ecosystem and form a complex network are called **food webs**.

- Predation occurs when one organism kills and eats another. A **predator** is an animal that hunts, kills, and eats other animals. The animals that are killed and eaten are called **prey**.

- Many organisms eat more than one type of food and are also a food source to other organisms. For instance, snakes are eaten by many different animals, such as large birds. They also eat other animals, such as mice.

A food web includes many feeding relationships within an ecosystem.

- Plants and animals depend on each other. All organisms interact with each other and with the nonliving environment.

In your notebook, list the concepts that you need to review. Then write down sources you can use to learn more about these concepts.

Humans and the Environment

The Living Environment: Key Idea 7

Earth's history is one of change. Some changes in the environment are due to natural events, such as floods and earthquakes. However, sometimes it is human activities, such as fighting wars and building dams, that change the living environment.

Vocabulary Terms acid rain, community, conservation, ecological succession, erosion, global warming, natural resource, nonrenewable resource, ozone layer, particulate, pollutant, pollution, population, recycle, renewable resource, soil

Put a check (✓) next to the concepts that you know.

Survival in Changing Environments All living things, including humans, depend on other living things and on nonliving parts of the environment for survival.

❏ An ecosystem is composed of **communities** of living organisms. A community is a group of different populations living in the same place and interacting with each other. A community interacts also with all the physical features, which are the nonliving parts of an area, such as land or water.

❏ A **population** is made up of all the members of a single species living in the same place and sharing resources.

❏ In all environments organisms interact with each other in many ways. They may compete for resources or come to depend on each other, as do predator and prey.

❏ Sometimes the environment may change suddenly. Other times the change is very gradual. **Ecological succession** is a very slow process of environmental change. Variations within members of a population may allow certain members to be better adapted to a changing environment. New species may replace others over time. This can lead to further changes in ecosystems.

Over time this meadow will change to a forest environment. As changes occur, the organisms that make up the community in the area will change.

❏ Overpopulation can harm the balance in the environment by using up resources.

Natural Resources The survival of living things on our planet depends on saving and protecting the Earth's resources.

❏ **Natural resources** are materials and energy that are used by living things.

❏ Natural resources must be used carefully and wisely. Wise use of natural resources is called **conservation.**

❏ Natural resources that can be reused or replaced are called **renewable resources.** Sunlight, air, water, and living things are examples of renewable resources.

- Some resources cannot be replaced or reused once they are used up. These resources, called **nonrenewable resources,** take millions of years to form. Oil, coal, natural gas, and minerals are some examples of nonrenewable resources.

- The supply of nonrenewable resources can be extended by **recycling.** Recycling is the process of reusing resources to make new products.

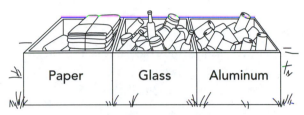

Recycling helps conserve nonrenewable resources.

- **Soil** is a nonrenewable resource. Because soil formation is a slow process, it is important to control soil **erosion.**

- Soil erosion can be prevented when farmers practice soil conservation methods such as contour plowing, planting trees as windbreaks, and strip-cropping.

Pollution Many living things are threatened by **pollution.** Pollution is anything that upsets the balance within ecosystems.

- Air pollution occurs when harmful substances, or **pollutants,** are released into the air. Cars and factories are two of the main sources of air pollution.

- Sulfur dioxide, nitrogen oxide, and carbon monoxide are all air pollutants by themselves. These materials can also combine with water in the air and fall to the ground as **acid rain.** Acid rain harms plant life and pollutes the water.

- **Particulates** are another kind of air pollutant. Particulates are tiny pieces of dust or soot in smoke.

- Damage to the Earth's **ozone layer** is another effect of air pollution. The ozone layer protects all life on Earth from harmful ultraviolet rays from the Sun. The ozone layer can be destroyed by CFCs (chlorofluorocarbons) and other chemicals.

- In a process known as **global warming,** temperatures could rise worldwide because of changes in the makeup of the atmosphere. The specific gases involved are called "greenhouse gases" and include carbon dioxide, water vapor, and methane.

- People can conserve fuel and reduce air pollution by walking, using buses or trains, or riding bicycles instead of driving cars.

- The disposing of waste by cities and towns is a major source of water pollution. Fertilizers and pesticides washed off farm fields by heavy rains are other sources. Chemical wastes from factories also pollute water and soil.

- The monitoring of pollutants is an important job of government. There are laws to prevent industry from dumping harmful wastes into the environment.

In your notebook, list the concepts that you need to review. Then write down sources you can use to learn more about these concepts.

The Earth and Space

The Physical Setting: Key Idea 1

The universe is made up of many kinds of objects, including the Earth and other bodies in the solar system. All objects in the universe are moving. Interactions among the objects in space, energy, and the forces that affect objects cause predictable, regular changes on Earth.

Vocabulary Terms asteroid, axis, comet, eclipse, elliptical, equator, force, globe, gravity, meteor, meteoroid, meteorite, moon, orbit, phase, revolution, rotation, solar system, star

Put a check (✓) next to the concepts that you know.

Our Local Neighborhood The **solar system** is home to the Sun and Earth, Earth's Moon, and all the other planets and moons, as well as other objects that orbit the Sun.

❑ The Sun is a **star.** Stars are huge balls of hot gases. They look small, like tiny points of light because they are so far away.

❑ The Sun is the central and largest body in the solar system. It is an average-sized yellow star.

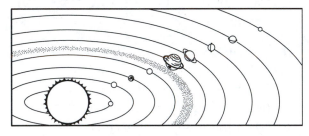

The solar system's inner planets are separated from its outer planets by an asteroid belt.

❑ After the Sun, the planets are the largest objects in our solar system. Each planet **orbits,** or moves in a closed, curved path around, the Sun in the same direction.

❑ The Earth is the third planet from the Sun. There are eight other planets in the solar system. Other objects in the solar system include **asteroids, comets,** and **meteoroids.**

❑ **Gravity** is a **force** that affects all objects in the universe. Gravity helps keep the planets in orbit around the Sun.

❑ Every object in the universe pulls on every other object. This pull is gravitational attraction.

❑ Most planets have **moons.** Moons are smaller bodies that orbit their planets. The Earth has one Moon. The Moon orbits the Earth about once a month.

❑ The part of the Moon that is lighted by the Sun changes during the orbit of the Moon around the Earth. This light is reflected to the Earth.

Phases of the Moon	
New Moon (Moon not visible)	●
Waxing crescent	◐
First quarter	◐
Waxing gibbous	◑
Full Moon	○
Waning gibbous	◑
Last quarter	◐
Waning crescent	◐

The amount of sunlight the Moon reflects to the Earth depends on where the Moon is in its orbit.

- The regular changes in the Moon's appearance during its orbit are called **phases**.

- Like planets and most other bodies, the Moon has an **elliptical** orbit. This means that the orbit is oval rather than round.

- Comets travel around the Sun in long, elliptical orbits. Comets are made of rock, dust, gas, and ice.

- Asteroids are large chunks of rock, metal, or both. Most asteroids are found in a "belt" between Mars and Jupiter.

- Smaller objects called meteoroids orbit the Sun. Some are as small as a grain of sand. When a meteoroid enters the Earth's atmosphere, it is called a **meteor** or shooting star. Meteors that strike the Earth's surface are called **meteorites**.

Movements in Space Most objects in the solar system have regular and predictable motions. These motions affect the length of a day and a year, the phases of the Moon, and other events and cycles.

- As it orbits the Sun, the Earth spins like a top on its **axis**. An axis is an imaginary line that runs through the center of the Earth from pole to pole. The Earth's axis is tilted to one side.

- The seasons are caused by the Earth's orbit around the Sun and the unchanging tilt of the Earth's axis.

- The angle of the Sun's rays changes with the season. In summer, although the Earth is actually farther from the Sun than in winter, the Sun's rays strike the Earth's surface more directly.

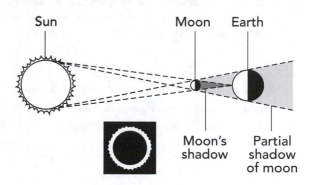

A solar eclipse occurs when the Moon passes between the Sun and the Earth.

- An **eclipse** occurs when one object passes into the shadow of another object. During a solar eclipse, the Earth passes into the Moon's shadow, so that the Sun cannot be seen. During a lunar eclipse, the Moon passes into the Earth's shadow.

- A **globe** is a sphere that has a map of the Earth on its surface. A globe can be used as a model of the Earth.

- The globe is cut into a northern half, or the Northern Hemisphere, and a southern half, the Southern Hemisphere, by an imaginary line called the **equator**.

- The **rotation** of the Earth every 24 hours produces the night-and-day cycle. For people on Earth, the rotation of the planet makes it seem as though the Sun, Moon, planets, and stars are orbiting the Earth.

- One complete movement, or orbit, of the Earth around the Sun is called a **revolution**. This process takes the Earth $365 \frac{1}{4}$ days and makes up our year.

- Different planets may have shorter or longer periods of rotation and revolution.

In your notebook, list the concepts that you need to review. Then write down sources you can use to learn more about these concepts.

The Interaction of Air, Land, and Water

The Physical Setting: Key Idea 2

The Earth is constantly changing and evolving as a result of interactions among the Earth's nonliving components: the air, land, and water.

Vocabulary Terms

atmosphere, climate, condensation, crust, earthquake, evaporation, glacier, greenhouse effect, hydrosphere, igneous rock, lithosphere, metamorphic rock, mineral, precipitation, rock cycle, sea-floor spreading, uplifting and folding, volcano, water cycle, weather, weathering

Put a check (✓) next to the concepts that you know.

Air A blanket of air, called the **atmosphere,** surrounds the Earth.

❑ The atmosphere is a mixture of gases. These gases are mostly nitrogen, oxygen, carbon dioxide, and water vapor.

❑ The atmosphere traps heat from the Sun and prevents some of it from going back into space. This is called the **greenhouse effect.**

❑ The different layers of the atmosphere have different characteristics.

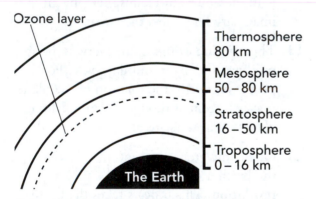

Ozone layer

Thermosphere
80 km

Mesosphere
50 – 80 km

Stratosphere
16 – 50 km

Troposphere
0 – 16 km

The Earth

Scientists divide the atmosphere into layers. However, there are really no sharp divisions between layers.

❑ The ozone layer protects the Earth from the Sun's ultraviolet radiation.

❑ The uneven heating of the Earth's land, air, and water causes **weather.** Many things contribute to the weather, including temperature, air pressure, and the amounts of water vapor in the air.

❑ Weather occurs in the troposphere, the layer of the atmosphere closest to the Earth.

Land The Earth's **crust** is made up mostly of rock, either bedrock or loose rock. The upper layer of the crust is called the **lithosphere.**

❑ Rocks are made up of different combinations of **minerals.** Minerals are natural substances that have specific properties.

❑ There are three kinds of rocks: **igneous,** sedimentary, and **metamorphic.** They are grouped by how they were formed. Igneous rocks come from lava flows. Sedimentary rocks come from deposits of sediments. Metamorphic rocks come from great pressure and heat that changes the chemistry of the original rocks.

❑ Rocks change types as they break down, wear away, get compressed, melt, or cool. This is called the **rock cycle.**

❑ Smaller rocks come from **weathering,** the breaking down of larger rocks by wind, rain, or ice.

❑ Soil comes from weathered rock and plant and animal remains. It also usually contains many living organisms.

Water Three-fourths of the Earth's surface is covered by a relatively thin layer of water called the **hydrosphere.**

❑ Water collects in lakes, oceans, soil, and underground. Some of it is frozen.

❑ Large sheets of ice that move slowly on the Earth's surface are called **glaciers.**

❑ The **water cycle** involves the movement of water from the surface of the Earth to the atmosphere and back.

❑ **Evaporation, condensation,** and **precipitation** are the three major processes in the water cycle.

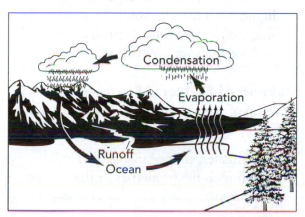

Less than 1 percent of all the water on Earth is involved in the water cycle at any one time. Most of the water on Earth actually remains in the ocean.

❑ Water is a solvent. It dissolves minerals and gases and carries them to the oceans or into underground water systems.

Reshaping the Earth's Surface The process of weathering slowly changes the Earth's surface. The interior of the Earth is hot. Movement of material and heat deep inside the Earth can cause sudden changes on its surface.

❑ Waves, wind, water, and glaciers gradually reshape the land.

❑ Surface layers of rock and soil are removed from some areas, transported, and deposited in other areas. This is erosion.

❑ Other gradual changes are **uplifting and folding** and **sea-floor spreading.**

❑ Movement of hot material inside the Earth can cause sections of the Earth's crust to suddenly shift. This may result in **earthquakes** or **volcanoes,** which change the land suddenly.

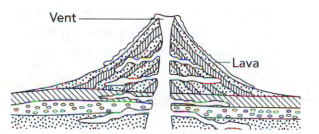

A volcano erupts through an opening called a vent.

❑ Gas and dust from large volcanic eruptions can change the atmosphere, which affects weather and **climate.**

❑ Mountains and ocean basins may also be formed from earthquakes and volcanic eruptions.

In your notebook, list the concepts that you need to review. Then write down sources you can use to learn more about these concepts.

Physical Properties of Matter

The Physical Setting: Key Idea 3

The universe is composed of matter. Different kinds of matter have different properties or characteristics.

Put a check (✓) next to the concepts that you know.

Properties of Matter Anything that takes up space and has **mass** is **matter**. Mass is the amount of matter in something.

❑ Substances have certain physical properties that identify them. Some of these properties include color, odor, phase at room temperature, mass, **density, solubility,** heat and electrical **conductivity,** hardness, and boiling and freezing points.

❑ Physical properties can be used to identify different materials and separate a mixture of substances into its components.

❑ There are three **states of matter:** solid, liquid, and gas. These are also called "phases."

❑ Changing the state of matter does not change what a substance is made of. When matter changes phase, heat energy is either absorbed or released.

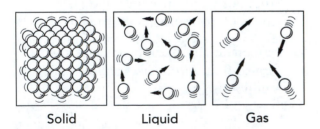

Solid   Liquid   Gas

Most matter exists in one or more of the three states of matter. Changing the state of matter results in molecules moving closer together or farther apart.

❑ A solid has a definite shape and volume. A liquid has a definite volume but takes the shape of its container. A gas has neither a definite shape nor a definite volume.

Makeup of Matter All matter on Earth is made up of **atoms.** Atoms are too small to be seen, even with a microscope.

❑ The smallest unit of matter that still contains all the properties of that matter is an atom.

❑ Matter made up of one kind of atom is an **element.** A **molecule** is made up of atoms that are chemically bound together.

❑ There more than 100 different elements found on Earth. These are listed in the **Periodic Table of the Elements**.

❑ Atoms and molecules are constantly in motion.

❑ Interactions among atoms often result in chemical reactions. Few elements are found in their pure form. They are usually found combined with other elements.

❑ Many substances **dissolve** in water. This may cause a chemical reaction.

❑ Heat makes molecules move faster. In a solid it results in melting.

- The removal of heat slows down the particles in a gas. This causes gases to condense and moves the atoms and molecules closer together to form a liquid.

- When enough heat is removed from a liquid, it freezes.

- Adding heat to a liquid by boiling gives the particles the energy to **evaporate,** forming a gas.

Physical and Chemical Changes Matter can be changed by either physical or chemical methods.

- A **mixture** is matter made up of two or more materials mixed together but not chemically joined.

- Mixtures can be separated by physical means. Mixing is an example of a **physical change.**

- During a physical change a substance keeps its chemical composition. Other examples of physical change include freezing, boiling, evaporation, tearing, and crushing.

- A magnetic substance can be removed from a mixture by means of a magnet. An insoluble substance can often be separated from a soluble substance by filtration or evaporation.

- A **compound** is a result of a **chemical change.** During a chemical change matter with a new chemical composition and new properties is formed. Examples of chemical changes include the burning of wood, cooking of food, rusting of iron, and souring of milk.

Burning is a chemical change. The wood molecules are irreversibly changed into other substances.

- The smallest particle in a compound that still has the chemical properties of the compound is the molecule.

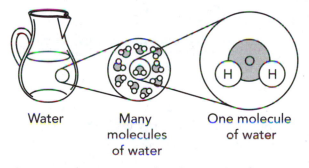

Water   Many molecules of water   One molecule of water

Compounds contain molecules made of different atoms. Water is made up of two hydrogen (H) atoms and one oxygen (O) atom.

- The **Law of the Conservation of Mass** states that during an ordinary chemical reaction, matter cannot be created or destroyed. It can only be rearranged. The total mass of the matter undergoing the reaction, or the **reactants,** equals the total mass of the **products** of the reaction.

- A **solution** is a mixture in which the particles of the substances are evenly mixed and cannot be separated by means such as filtering.

In your notebook, list the concepts that you need to review. Then write down sources you can use to learn more about these concepts.

Forms of Energy

The Physical Setting: Key Idea 4

Energy can neither be created nor destroyed. However, it can take many forms. The transfer from one form to another usually produces heat.

Vocabulary Terms chemical energy, circuits, conductor, current, electrical energy, electromagnetic spectrum, electrons, energy, fossil fuel, fusion, geothermal energy, heat energy, hydroelectric energy, infrared light, kinetic energy, light energy, mechanical energy, nuclear energy, nuclear fission, opaque, potential energy, reflection, refraction, resistor, solar energy, spectrum, translucent, transparent, ultraviolet light, vibration, visible light, wavelength

Put a check (✓) next to the concepts that you know.

Energy There is energy in all things, whether they are moving or standing still.

❏ **Energy** is the ability to do work or cause change.

❏ Energy can be stored. Energy stored in matter is called **potential energy**. The amount of potential energy in an object depends on its position or condition.

❏ The energy of motion is called kinetic energy. **Kinetic energy** is energy being used instead of stored.

❏ The amount of kinetic energy in an object depends on the object's mass, speed, and direction. The kinetic energy of moving objects is also called **mechanical energy.**

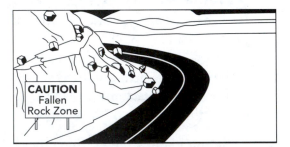

The falling rocks have kinetic energy.

❏ The main source of energy on Earth is the Sun. This energy, called **solar energy,** provides the Earth with both **light energy** and **heat energy.**

❏ Heat energy is energy in the form of moving molecules. Hot objects contain more heat energy than cold objects.

❏ Energy stored in molecules is called **chemical energy.** When molecules react with each other, the energy stored in them may be released. Cars use the chemical energy stored in gasoline. Your body uses the chemical energy stored in food.

❏ The energy stored in the nucleus of an atom is called **nuclear energy.** This energy is released when the nucleus is split. The splitting of a nucleus is called **nuclear fission.** Nuclear energy is also released by combining the nuclei of two atoms. This is called **nuclear fusion.**

❏ **Fossil fuels** are made up of organisms that died millions of years ago. Fossil fuels contain stored energy. Coal, oil, and gas are fossil fuels that are burned to provide energy. They are nonrenewable sources of energy.

❏ When energy changes from one form to another, some of it becomes heat.

Light and Sound Light and sound energy move in waves.

❏ Light energy travels through space at the speed of about 186,000 miles (300,000 kilometers) per second. Light is the fastest moving thing in the universe.

❏ Light can pass right through a **transparent** object, like a window. An **opaque** object, like a wall, absorbs most of the light hitting it. A **translucent** object, like frosted glass, allows some light to pass through it.

❏ Light rays may be bent at angles as they pass from one substance to another. This bending is called **refraction**. When light bounces off an object, **reflection** occurs. Mirrors are good reflectors.

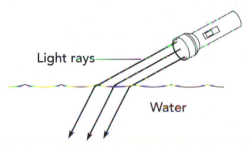

Light rays are refracted as they move from the air into the water.

❏ Light is composed of many different **wavelengths.** The wavelengths of light we can see are called **visible light**. The different wavelengths of visible light form a band of seven colors called a **spectrum**. A rainbow is an example of a spectrum.

❏ Some wavelengths, called **ultraviolet light,** are too short to see. Other wavelengths, called **infrared light,** are too long to see. Visible and invisible light, along with other forms of radiation, make up the **electromagnetic spectrum.**

❏ Sound is produced by matter that vibrates. **Vibrations** travel in waves through different materials at different speeds. Sound vibrations travel better through solids than through gases or liquids.

Electrical Energy Energy in the form of moving **electrons** is called **electrical energy.** Electrons are negatively charged particles inside atoms. Lightning is a form of electrical energy.

❏ Some materials, such as copper, allow the flow of electrons to pass easily. These materials are called **conductors. Resistors** oppose the flow of electrons.

❏ **Currents** of electricity flowing in the same direction are called **circuits**. A circuit always has a source of energy, such as a battery.

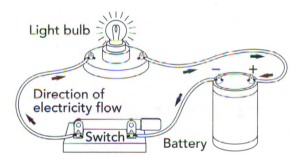

This closed electrical circuit connects a battery to a light.

❏ Many sources can provide electrical energy. **Hydroelectric energy** is electrical energy from the kinetic energy of water falling behind a dam.

❏ The heat in hot rock deep inside the Earth is called **geothermal energy.** This energy can be used to heat homes and produce electricity.

In your notebook, list the concepts that you need to review. Then write down sources you can use to learn more about these concepts.

Forces and Motion

The Physical Setting: Key Idea 5

The interaction of matter and energy creates forces, which result in changes in motion. All objects on Earth have a number of forces acting on them.

Vocabulary Terms compound machine, effort force, First Law of Motion, friction, fulcrum, inclined plane, inertia, lever, lubricant, machine, magnet, magnetism, mass, pulley, resistance force, screw, Second Law of Motion, simple machine, Third Law of Motion, wedge, wheel and axle, work

Put a check (✓) next to the concepts that you know.

Force and Motion A force is any push or pull on an object. Common forces include gravity and **magnetism**.

❑ Electric currents and **magnets** can exert a force on each other. A magnet is a piece of metal that attracts iron or steel.

❑ Motion results from a change in the position of an object. It is always discussed with respect to some other object or point.

❑ To describe motion, we must usually include speed, or how fast something moves, and direction. Motion can be measured and shown on a graph.

❑ The tendency of an object to stay at rest or in motion unless acted upon by an outside force is called **inertia**.

❑ When an object is at rest, all the forces acting on it are balanced. When an object moves, the forces are unbalanced. An object moves in the direction of the greatest force acting on it.

Laws of Motion Forces change the motion of objects in ways that can be predicted.

❑ The **First Law of Motion** states that an object in motion stays in motion, and an object at rest stays at rest, unless another force acts on it. This is also known as the Law of Inertia.

❑ The **Second Law of Motion** states that a force acting on an object causes the object to accelerate in the direction of the force. Acceleration is a change in speed or direction. The object's acceleration is in direct proportion to the forces, as long as the object's mass remains constant.

❑ The **Third Law of Motion** states that for every force applied to an object, there is an equal and opposite reaction force.

❑ **Friction** is a force that slows or prevents motion. This is the force that stops skateboards from continuing to roll.

❑ Three types of friction are rolling friction, sliding friction, and fluid friction.

❑ A **lubricant** is a substance that reduces friction.

The rolling friction of the bicycle wheels can be overcome by force and lubricants.

Work Work occurs when a force moves an object through a distance.

❑ There are two forces involved when doing work. The force applied is the **effort force.** The force that must be overcome when doing work is the **resistance force.**

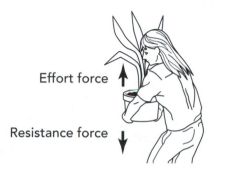

Effort force

Resistance force

When you lift a load, such as a potted plant, the resistance force is gravity. The greater the load's mass, the greater the resistance force.

Machines Machines are tools or devices used to do work. Some machines have many parts, some only one or two.

❑ A **simple machine** is a machine that changes the size or the direction of an applied force. Most simple machines, like the ones described here, work with only one movement.

❑ A **lever** is a bar that turns around a fixed point, or **fulcrum.** A seesaw is a lever. A **pulley** is a grooved wheel with a rope or a chain running along the groove. A pulley works just like a lever. The wheel is the fulcrum and the rope is the bar.

❑ A **wheel and axle** is a simple machine consisting of two wheels of different sizes that rotate together. A wheel and axle works like a lever attached to a shaft.

❑ An **inclined plane** is a sloping surface used to raise objects. A **wedge** is made of two inclined planes placed back to back. Knives, axes, needles, and can openers are all wedges. A **screw** is an inclined plane wrapped around a cylinder.

❑ A **compound machine** is made of two or more simple machines.

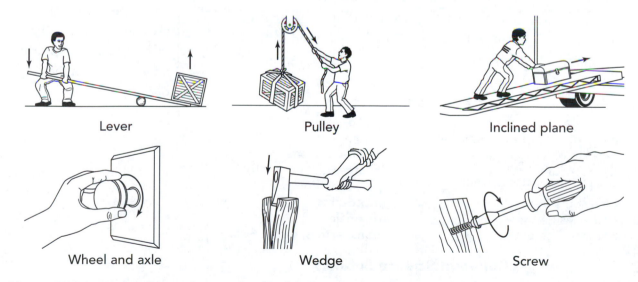

Lever

Pulley

Inclined plane

Wheel and axle

Wedge

Screw

Most machines are made up of two or more of the six simple machines.

In your notebook, list the concepts that you need to review. Then write down sources you can use to learn more about these concepts.

CHAPTER 2

Decoding Multiple-Choice Questions

Many test questions provide multiple-choice answers. Of course, if you know the science content being tested, answering these questions should not be very difficult. However, even if you think you know the content, you will increase your chances of choosing the right answer by using the strategies that follow. They will teach you how to interpret, or decode, both the questions and the answer choices.

Read Carefully!

Read the question and answer choices carefully to avoid giving a wrong answer to a question you know. Follow these tips:

- **Be sure you know what the question is asking.** If you read a question and all the answer choices seem to make sense, you may have misunderstood the question. Reread the question, and be sure you know what is being asked.

- **Look for key words such as *ALL, NOT,* or *NONE.*** These will help you quickly eliminate some of the choices.

- **Use prefixes and suffixes to help you understand unfamiliar vocabulary.** A *prefix* is found at the beginning of a word. A *suffix* is found at the end of a word. Prefixes and suffixes change or add meaning to *root* words. Below is a list of prefixes and suffixes commonly used in science.

> ✏️ **Test Tip**
>
> Key words will not usually be indicated by **CAPITAL** letters or **bold-faced** or *italic* type. If you are allowed to write on the test, underline key words if they appear in the question.

Common Science Prefixes

anti- against; opposite
auto- directed from within; self
bio- life or living organism
de- reversal or removal
di-, bi- two
ecto- outside
endo- inside
hetero- different

homo- same
in-, im- not
mono-, uni- one
photo- light
poly-, multi- many
proto- first
re- again
trans- across, beyond

Common Science Suffixes

-able, -ible—capable of
-ance, -ence—condition, state, or quality of
-ant, -ent—being or causing
-meter—means of measuring
-sion, -tion—the act, process, or result of
-yze, -ise, -ize—to do or to make
-trop, -tropo—turn, turning, change

Examples The following questions can help you understand what is meant by reading carefully.

> **1** Animals that do not have backbones are
>
> | 1 vertebrates | 3 mammals |
> |---|---|
> | 2 invertebrates | 4 reptiles |

Content Clue

Invertebrates make up over 90 percent of the animal **kingdom**.

Step 1 By carefully reading the question, you will see that it contains the key word NOT. To answer this question correctly, you need to identify animals that do NOT have backbones.

Step 2 Start eliminating possibilities right away. What do you know about choice 3, mammals? What animals do you know that are mammals? Do they have backbones? Humans are mammals. So are cats, dogs, and horses. You know that all these animals have backbones. Therefore, 3 is not the correct answer. Use the same process to eliminate choice 4.

Step 3 Now look at choice 2, invertebrates. The chart of prefixes shows that the prefix *in-* means "not." *In*vertebrates are *not* vertebrates. In other words, invertebrates do *not* have vertebrae. Vertebrae are bones in your back. So animals that do NOT have backbones are invertebrates, choice 2.

> **2** The tendency of plants to turn toward light is the result of
>
> | 1 transpiration | 3 geotropism |
> |---|---|
> | 2 photosynthesis | 4 phototropism |

Test Tip

Make sure you read *all* possible answers before choosing one.

Step 1 All four of the choices for this question refer to plant processes. Look at the prefixes and suffixes in these words. The prefix *photo-* means "light." Neither choice 1 nor choice 3 includes this prefix. So, you can eliminate those choices.

Step 2 Now look at the remaining choices. In choice 2, the word part *synthesis* means "to make," which doesn't fit the question. In choice 4, the suffix *-trop* means "turning." So *phototropism* means "turning toward the light." The correct choice is 4.

Rephrase the Question

If you have trouble understanding a question, try putting it in your own words. This can help you see where the problem is. It may also help you recall important science content.

Test Tip

Another way to rephrase a question is to make it into a statement with the answer at the end.

Example   Rephrasing this question should help you answer it.

3 Marble forms when limestone is subjected to heat and
pressure. What type of rock is marble?

    1 sedimentary   3 igneous

    2 metamorphic   4 mineral

Step 1   Simplify the question by stating it in your own words.
Possibilities include "What type of rock is formed by heat and
pressure?" and "What type of rock is formed by changing another
type of rock?" These new ways of asking the question may help you
recall that there are three types of rock— igneous, sedimentary, and
metamorphic. These are grouped by the way they are formed. Once
you know this, you can eliminate choice 4.

Step 2   Now you can use prefixes, suffixes, and root words to help
you with the other choices. The word *sedimentary* includes the word
sediment. Sedimentary rocks are formed from sediments that are
carried by water to new places and deposited. They are not formed
by heat and pressure, so you can eliminate choice 1. In *metamorphic*,
the prefix *meta-* means "change," and the root *morph* means "form."
Metamorphic rock results from changing the form of a rock. Marble
results from changing the form of limestone. Therefore, you know
that the correct answer is 2.

Narrow Your Choices

Careful reading and thinking about each answer choice will help
you avoid making mistakes. Follow these tips:

- **Eliminate any answers that are obviously wrong.** Many
  questions include choices that are clearly wrong. Eliminating
  these choices from the start can keep you from being confused
  by them.

- **Recall facts that help you narrow the choices.** Think of all the
  facts you know about the concept being tested. You probably
  know more than you think you do. You may be able to eliminate
  even more wrong answers.

- **Think about what you know that applies to the question.**
  Search your mind to see if you can think of any situation in your
  daily life that might provide clues that will help you in narrowing
  the choices.

Test Tip

Once you eliminate a
choice, cross it out to help
you focus on the other
choices.

Content Clue

Diamonds are a type of
metamorphic rock. They
are formed when deposits
of carbon are subjected to
great heat and pressure
deep inside the Earth's
crust.

Examples These questions show you how to apply the strategies you have just read.

4 As the temperature of water rises from 25°C to 35°C, the molecules of water
    1 move faster
    2 move closer together
    3 decompose to form hydrogen and oxygen
    4 react with one another to form a new substance

Step 1 Think about what you know about water. Water is a liquid at both 25°C and 35°C. It does not decompose or chemically react by itself at these temperatures. Therefore, you can eliminate choices 3 and 4.

Step 2 Now review what you know about temperature. Maybe you recall that heat causes a liquid to turn into a gas and that gas molecules move faster than the molecules in a liquid. Therefore, temperature measures the average kinetic energy of the molecules of a substance. As the temperature of a substance rises, its molecules gain kinetic energy. This means they move faster. So, as the temperature of the water rises, its molecules move faster, choice 1.

Content Clue

Water freezes at 0°C and boils at 100°C.

5 What causes the seasons on Earth?
    1 The Earth rotates on its axis once a day.
    2 The Earth revolves around the Sun once every year.
    3 The Earth's orbit around the Sun is an ellipse, so at some times of the year the Earth is closer to the Sun than at other times.
    4 The Earth is tilted on its axis, so as it orbits the Sun, the Sun's rays hit it more directly at some times of the year than at other times.

Step 1 Read the choices. Each statement is true. However, only one of them describes the cause of the seasons. You can eliminate choice 1 because the time involved is too small. Rotation is the cause of day and night, not the cause of seasons. Choice 2 gives part of the answer but not the whole answer.

Step 2 Look at choice 3. It is not an incorrect statement. However, it is misleading. The Earth is actually closer to the Sun in the Nothern hemisphere in winter than it is in summer. The correct answer is choice 4.

Test Tip

Make sure your choice answers the question. A choice may be a true statement and still not answer the question.

Test Tip

If you are still not sure, make an educated guess. In multiple-choice questions, one of the choices is the correct answer, so you always have a chance of being right.

Practice

Living and Nonliving Things

Each question is followed by four choices. Mark the choice that is the best answer.

1 What do plant cells have that animal cells do not?
   1 chromosomes and DNA
   2 cell membranes and mitochondria
   3 nuclei and membrane-bound organelles
   4 chloroplasts and cell walls

2 The phylum that includes mammals, birds, fish, reptiles, and amphibians is
   1 Echinoderm   3 Chordata
   2 Animalia   4 Vertebrate

> ✏️ **Test Tip**
>
> Reread the question to be sure you know what it is asking. The answer to question 2 is the name of a **phylum.**

3 Fungi are organisms that
   1 are unicellular
   2 are classified in the plant kingdom
   3 require light to grow
   4 break down dead matter and absorb useful elements from it

> 📖 **Content Clue**
>
> Mushrooms are examples of **fungi**. Scientists used to classify fungi as plants. Today, fungi are classified in their own **kingdom**.

4 Nonvascular plants do not have
   1 roots   3 transportation tubes
   2 leaves   4 chlorophyll

5 An organ that is not part of the digestive system is the
   1 stomach
   2 liver
   3 kidney
   4 small intestine

> ✏️ **Test Tip**
>
> Look for key words such as *all*, *not*, or *none*.

6 A chemical from a gland that affects other body parts is
   1 stomach acid   3 saliva
   2 a hormone   4 cytoplasm

Practice

Genetic Information

Each question is followed by four choices. Mark the choice that is the best answer.

1 Hereditary information is passed from one generation to the next by

  1 chromosomes   3 traits

  2 Punnett squares   4 cytoplasm

2 A section of DNA that contains the blueprint for a single trait is

  1 a chromosome   3 a molecule

  2 a gene   4 an organelle

3 Humans have 46 chromosomes. How many of a child's chromosomes come from its mother?

  1 12   3 32

  2 23   4 46

 **Test Tip**

Eliminate any answers that are obviously wrong, such as 3.

Use the diagrams below to help you answer questions 4 and 5.

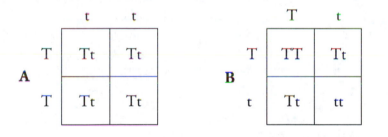

4 Mendel first crossed pea plants with the gene for tallness (T) with pea plants with the gene for shortness (t). What does Punnett square A tell you about the offspring?

  1 All offspring were tall.

  2 All offspring were short.

  3 Half the offspring were tall and half were short.

  4 Three-fourths were tall and one-fourth were short.

Content Clues

Tallness is a **dominant trait** in pea plants. Shortness is a **recessive trait**.

Only individuals with two **genes** for a recessive trait will show that **trait**.

5 What does Punnett square B tell you about the offspring of this experiment?

  1 All offspring were tall.

  2 All offspring were short.

  3 Half the offspring were tall and half were short.

  4 Three-fourths were tall and one-fourth were short.

Practice

Change Over Time

Each question is followed by four choices. Mark the choice that is the best answer.

1 The two processes that produce variations in living things are
1 sexual and asexual reproduction
2 asexual reproduction and changes in the environment
3 mutation and changes in the environment
4 sexual reproduction and mutation

Content Clue

An **organism** produced by **asexual reproduction,** or one parent, has exactly the same **traits** as its parent.

2 A species becomes extinct when
1 changes in the environment force organisms to move to a new location
2 predators kill all the members of a species in a given area
3 all members of the species have died
4 all the natural enemies of the species have died

3 After a very cold, dry winter, which wolves are most likely to survive and have offspring?
1 those with dark fur
2 those with white fur
3 those with thick fur
4 those with thin fur

Test Tip

Rephrase question 3 in your own words, for example: *Which wolves are most likely to survive a very cold, dry winter?*

4 The fossil record shows that
1 all types of organisms that have ever lived are still alive today
2 Earth's climate has been the same for millions of years
3 many species of organisms that once lived are now extinct
4 dinosaurs died out because they could not protect themselves from humans

5 One example of variation and natural selection taking place today is
1 animals becoming extinct because of loss of habitat
2 strains of bacteria becoming resistant to antibiotics
3 organisms such as sheep being cloned
4 corn plants producing better-quality corn

Test Tip

Try to recall facts that help you narrow the choices. For question 5, you might recall news stories reporting that cloning produces exact copies. So cloning cannot be an example of **variation.**

Practice

Reproduction and Development

Each question is followed by four choices. Mark the choice that is the best answer.

1 Which of these is a type of sexual reproduction in plants?
1 grafting one plant onto another
2 growing a new plant from runners
3 growing a new plant from a cutting
4 growing a new plant from a seed

2 In sexual reproduction each new individual develops from
1 a fertilized egg   3 a sperm cell
2 spores   4 buds

3 In the pupa stage of a moth's life cycle, the organism
1 eats leaves and grows
2 lives inside a cocoon, changing its shape
3 flies and drinks nectar
4 lays eggs

4 After mitosis, each daughter cell has _____ of chromosomes as the parent cell.
1 one-fourth the number
2 one-half the number
3 the same number
4 twice the number

5 After meiosis, each new cell has _____ of chromosomes as the parent cell.
1 one-fourth the number
2 one-half the number
3 the same number
4 twice the number

6 Meiosis in a male results in the formation of
1 egg cells   3 liver cells
2 sperm cells   4 brain cells

Content Clue

Grafting is one way of producing a new plant from only one parent. The new plant is identical to its parent plant.

Test Tip

Recalling diagrams can be easier than recalling facts. Try to picture the diagram of the moth's **life cycle** to answer question 3.

Content Clue

Meiosis is a type of cell division during which reproductive cells are formed.

Practice

Meeting Daily Needs

Each question is followed by four choices. Mark the choice that is the best answer.

1 Fungi can best be classified as
 1 producers
 2 photosynthetic organisms
 3 secondary consumers
 4 decomposers

 **Test Tip**

Define each science word and try to name examples of each one.

2 What role do plants play in an ecosystem?
 1 producers
 2 primary consumers
 3 secondary consumers
 4 decomposers

3 Which of the following animals is an endotherm?
 1 lobster   3 snake
 2 frog   4 chimpanzee

Content Clue

The prefix *endo-* means "inside," and the root word *-therm* means "heat." Endotherms get their body heat from inside. Another term for endotherm is **warm-blooded.**

4 Nutrients the body needs for the growth and repair of cells are
 1 carbohydrates   3 proteins
 2 fats   4 vitamins

5 A person who takes in 2,800 Calories a day and uses 2,300 Calories a day will most likely
 1 gain weight   3 grow taller
 2 lose weight   4 lose muscle mass

 **Content Clue**

Calories measure the amount of **energy** in food.

6 Which of the following is not harmful to the development of an unborn child during pregnancy?
 1 alcohol   3 pizza
 2 tobacco   4 cocaine

7 The breaking down of food by an organism is called
 1 digestion   3 respiration
 2 excretion   4 circulation

Practice

Energy in Ecosystems

Each question is followed by four choices. Mark the choice that is the best answer.

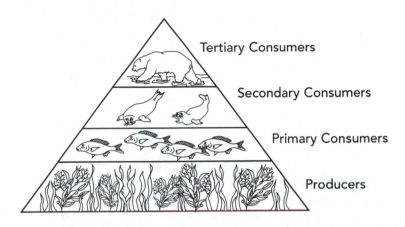

Content Clue

Each level of the **energy pyramid** has about 10 percent of the **energy** of the level below it.

1 In the energy pyramid shown above, energy flows

  1 from right to left   3 from top to bottom

  2 from left to right   4 from bottom to top

2 Most of the energy in this energy pyramid is found at the

  1 top level   3 second level below the top

  2 first level below the top   4 bottom level

3 Which of the following statements about this ecosystem cannot be inferred from the energy pyramid?

  1 There are more fish than seals.

  2 More energy is in the sea plants than in the fish.

  3 Polar bears eat seals.

  4 Polar bears eat sea plants.

Test Tip

Check each choice in question 3 against what you can see in the energy pyramid.

4 In the process of photosynthesis, plants use

  1 water and sugar to make protein

  2 carbon dioxide and oxygen to make protein

  3 water and carbon dioxide to make sugar and oxygen

  4 water and oxygen to make sugar and carbon dioxide

5 The chemical in green plants that allows them to carry out photosynthesis is

  1 chlorophyll   3 glucose

  2 sodium chloride   4 oxygen

Practice

Humans and the Environment

Each question is followed by four choices. Mark the choice that is the best answer.

1 An ecosystem is
   1 all the animals living in a particular environment
   2 a community of living things
   3 animals interacting with plants
   4 all the living and nonliving things that interact in an area

2 In parasitism two organisms live together and
   1 both organisms benefit
   2 one organism benefits while the other is harmed
   3 one organism benefits while the other is unaffected
   4 neither organism benefits

3 Which of the following human actions would benefit the surrounding ecosystem?
   1 draining wetlands
   2 releasing waste water into a river
   3 carpooling
   4 urban sprawl

4 Acid rain can do all the following except
   1 clean streams
   2 destroy soil
   3 eat away statues and buildings
   4 kill plants and animals in lakes

5 Which of these is a renewable resource?
   1 aluminum   3 wood
   2 oil   4 soil

6 Particulates pollute the environment by sending into the air
   1 soot   3 carbon dioxide
   2 gasoline   4 CFCs

✎ Test Tip

Always look for the *best* answer to the question. A few of the answers might seem possible, but one should stand out as better than the rest.

✎ Test Tip

Think about situations relevant to the question. Try to recall examples of **parasites** you have heard of. For example, maybe you know that athlete's foot is caused by a parasite.

📖 Content Clue

A **renewable resource** is one that can be replaced within the human life span.

Practice

The Earth and Space

Each question is followed by four choices. Mark the choice that is the best answer.

1 In our solar system the planet closest to the Sun is
   1 Mercury   3 Earth
   2 Venus   4 Mars

 **Test Tip**

Eliminate answers that are obviously wrong. You know that the Earth is not the planet closest to the Sun, so you can eliminate choice 3 for question 1.

2 The length of time it takes the Earth to orbit the Sun is called a
   1 day   3 month
   2 week   4 year

3 The length of time it takes the Earth to rotate once on its axis is called a
   1 day   3 month
   2 week   4 year

4 When we look at the Moon, the light we see comes from
   1 the Moon   3 the Sun
   2 the Earth   4 faraway stars

 **Content Clue**

Neither the Moon nor the Earth generates its own light.

5 The major force that keeps the Earth in orbit around the Sun is
   1 rotation   3 revolution
   2 gravity   4 elliptical motion

6 A solar eclipse occurs when
   1 the Earth's shadow falls on the Moon
   2 the Earth's shadow falls on the Sun
   3 the Moon's shadow falls on the Earth
   4 the Moon's shadow falls on the Sun

7 Stars are
   1 the same as asteroids
   2 huge balls of hot gases
   3 in orbit around the Sun
   4 in elliptical orbits around planets

Practice

The Interaction of Air, Land, and Water

Each question is followed by four choices. Mark the choice that is the best answer.

1 Sedimentary rock is formed by
  1 erosion and deposition
  2 heat and pressure
  3 melting and solidification
  4 evaporation and condensation

2 The layer of the atmosphere in which most weather occurs is the
  1 troposphere   3 mesosphere
  2 stratosphere   4 ionosphere

3 The gas that makes up most of the Earth's atmosphere is
  1 oxygen   3 nitrogen
  2 hydrogen   4 carbon dioxide

4 The energy that causes the Earth's plates to move comes from
  1 the Sun   3 the water cycle
  2 inside the Earth 4 the rock cycle

5 Two of the Earth's plates slipping past each other at a transform fault boundary can cause
  1 a volcanic eruption   3 a subduction zone
  2 an earthquake   4 a convergent zone

6 Molecules of water on the Earth
  1 go to the bottom of the ocean and stay there forever
  2 evaporate and end up in outer space
  3 cycle over and over again through the Earth's surface, organisms, and atmosphere
  4 freeze into the polar ice caps and stay there forever

7 The process in which rocks change as they break down, wear away, get compressed, melt, or cool is called
  1 erosion   3 the rock cycle
  2 deposition   4 volcanism

Content Clues

Sediment is rock, sand, or dirt carried by wind, water, or ice to a new place.

The prefix *tropo-* means "turning" or "changing." *Stratus* is a Latin root meaning "spread out," and *meso* comes from Latin for "middle."

✏️ **Test Tip**

Make sure you know what the question is asking. Where are the plates that move, and what causes them to move?

Content Clue

The San Andreas Fault in California is the boundary for two **plates** that sometimes slip past each other.

Practice

Physical Properties of Matter

Each question is followed by four choices. Mark the choice that is the best answer.

1 Study the diagram. What is the density of the block of wood?

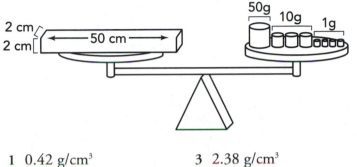

1 0.42 g/cm³   3 2.38 g/cm³

2 0.84 g/cm³   4 42 g/cm³

2 All matter is made of particles called
   1 cells   3 atoms
   2 element   4 photons

3 Which of the following is a chemical change?
   1 sugar dissolving in water
   2 wood burning in a fireplace
   3 magnetizing a steel screwdriver
   4 boiling water on a stove

4 The molecules in liquid water _____ than the molecules in ice.
   1 move faster   3 have more mass
   2 move more slowly 4 have less mass

5 The noble gases helium, neon, argon, krypton, xenon, and radon
   1 react easily with water
   2 burn brightly when heated in air
   3 explode when put in water
   4 react only under extreme conditions

6 Oxygen is
   1 an element   3 a mixture
   2 a compound   4 a solution

Content Clue

Density = **mass**/volume. Find the volume of a block by multiplying length times width times height.

Test Tip

Read carefully! Question 2 is asking for the name of the particles that make up *all* matter, not just living things.

Content Clue

A **chemical change** produces a new substance.

Practice

Forms of Energy

Each question is followed by four choices. Mark the choice that is the best answer.

Use the diagram to answer Questions 1 and 2.

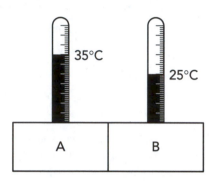

1 Heat will move
  1 by convection from Block A to Block B
  2 by convection from Block B to Block A
  3 by conduction from Block A to Block B
  4 by conduction from Block B to Block A

Content Clue

Convection is the process that moves heat through liquids and gases. It does not move heat through solids.

2 The transfer of heat between Blocks A and B will stop when
  1 Block B reaches 35°C
  2 Block A reaches 25°C
  3 Blocks A and B reach the same temperature
  4 Blocks A and B lose all their heat

Test Tip

Think about situations that apply to the question. When you look in a mirror, you see your **reflection.** Reflection, not **refraction**, occurs when light bounces off a surface, so you can eliminate choice 1 in question 3.

3 Refraction occurs when
  1 light bounces off a surface
  2 light moves from one medium to another, bending
  3 light is absorbed by an object
  4 some wavelengths of light are absorbed by an object while others are reflected

4 Which energy conversion is represented by a lighted incandescent bulb?
  1 electrical energy is changed to chemical energy
  2 electrical energy is changed to light and heat
  3 chemical energy is changed to light and heat
  4 chemical energy is changed to electrical energy

Content Clue

To turn on a light, you have to switch on the electricity. The energy that goes into the light bulb is electrical energy.

Practice

Forces and Motion

Each question is followed by four choices. Mark the choice that is the best answer.

1 An object's motion is the result of
  1 friction and inertia
  2 inertia and gravity
  3 gravity and speed
  4 all the forces acting on the object

2 Mary is standing on a train moving east at 10 km per hour. Alicia is sitting on a train that passes in the opposite direction at 30 km per hour. From Mary's point of view, how fast is Alicia moving?
  1 10 km per hour   3 30 km per hour
  2 20 km per hour   4 40 km per hour

3 An electromagnet works because
  1 an electric current produces a magnetic field
  2 a magnetic field produces an electric current
  3 an electric current produces friction
  4 a magnetic field produces friction

4 Why does the Earth exert a greater gravitational pull on the Moon than the Sun does?
  1 The Earth is smaller than the Sun.
  2 The Earth is larger than the Sun.
  3 The Moon is closer to the Sun.
  4 The Moon is closer to the Earth.

5 A ball is rolling in a straight line on level ground. It slows down and stops. What force stops it?
  1 gravity   3 inertia
  2 friction   4 centripetal force

6 When you lift a load, the resistance force is
  1 magnetism   3 electricity
  2 inertia   4 gravity

Content Clue

An object at rest tends to stay at rest and an object in **motion** tends to stay in motion in a straight line until an outside **force** acts on it.

Test Tip

From Mary's point of view, Alicia is moving [10−(−30)] km per hr.

Test Tip

Recall facts that help you narrow the choices. Think about what an electromagnet looks like and how you make it work.

Test Tip

Eliminate answers that are obviously wrong. In question 4, the Earth is not larger than the Sun, so choice 2 is wrong. The Moon is not closer to the Sun than it is to the Earth, so choice 3 is wrong. Choices 1 and 4 are both true statements, but only one of them answers the question.

CHAPTER 3

Working with Diagrams

Much of what you learn in school is presented as written text. However, information can also be presented in other ways. *Visuals* such as diagrams, photographs, and maps are also important ways to communicate scientific information or data.

Reading Diagrams

A diagram is a labeled illustration. Diagrams use pictures to show information such as the parts of an object or stages of a process. A diagram may show information that is described in writing. It may be used in place of words to provide you with information about a subject.

Diagrams That Show an Object

The first step in reading a diagram is to identify the subject or topic of the diagram. Often this information is presented in a title. Sometimes knowing the title is all you need to answer a question correctly.

Example Look at the title of the diagram shown below. What is the subject or topic of the diagram? _____

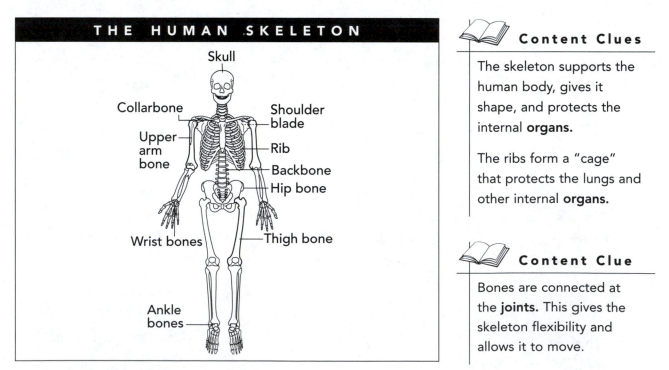

THE HUMAN SKELETON

Skull
Collarbone
Shoulder blade
Upper arm bone
Rib
Backbone
Hip bone
Wrist bones
Thigh bone
Ankle bones

About 206 bones make up the human skeleton.

Content Clues

The skeleton supports the human body, gives it shape, and protects the internal **organs.**

The ribs form a "cage" that protects the lungs and other internal **organs.**

Content Clue

Bones are connected at the **joints.** This gives the skeleton flexibility and allows it to move.

The labels on diagrams are words or phrases that provide details about the subject of the diagram, such as the names of different parts of the object being shown. In most cases lines connect the labels to the parts they are identifying.

Look at the labels on the diagram of the skeleton. What kinds of information or details do they give you about the skeleton? _____

Many diagrams also have a third part, called a caption. The caption usually appears below the diagram. A caption is a sentence or a phrase that gives you more information about the diagram shown. Captions often sum up what the diagram shows. What does the caption for the illustration on page 42 tell you? _____

✏️ **Test Tip**

Diagrams are usually drawn to scale. That is, they show the relative sizes or distances of objects in the diagram.

Diagrams That Compare and Contrast

Sometimes you might be given a diagram that compares and contrasts.

Example The following diagram compares the Fahrenheit temperature scale with the Celsius temperature scale.

📖 **Content Clue**

The **Celsius** scale is part of the metric system. It is based on the **boiling point** and **freezing point** of water. The Celsius scale is the only temperature scale used on the examination.

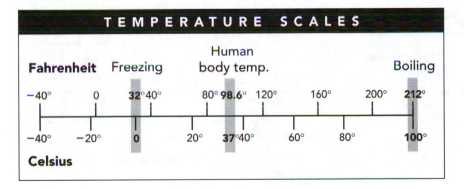

To tell someone how to convert from Fahrenheit to Celsius, you would need to write a procedure such as this one:

1. Subtract 32 from the Fahrenheit number.

2. Divide your answer by 9.

3. Multiply your answer by 5.

This procedure may be useful, but it does not give you a clear picture of how the two scales are related. By showing them together on a diagram, you can more easily see, for example, that 0 degrees Celsius and 32 degrees Fahrenheit are both the freezing point of water. What is the boiling point of water on each scale? _____

_____

This diagram shows the relationship between the two temperature scales. It could also be used as a tool for converting from one scale to the other. How do you think using the diagram to convert would compare in terms of accuracy to actually doing the calculations? _____

_____

Diagrams That Show a Process

Some diagrams show information about a process.

Example The following diagram shows the life cycle of a butterfly. What part of the diagram tells you the subject of the diagram? _____

This diagram has arrows in addition to labels. Symbols such as arrows are often used in diagrams to indicate processes or change. Look at the labels and the symbols. What do these labels tell you must occur before the caterpillar becomes a butterfly? _____

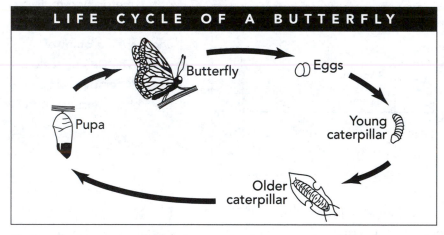

LIFE CYCLE OF A BUTTERFLY

Butterfly · Eggs · Young caterpillar · Older caterpillar · Pupa

During the process called metamorphosis, an egg hatches into a caterpillar. The caterpillar will eventually become a butterfly and lay its own eggs.

Test Tip

In a cycle or flowchart diagram, the direction of the arrows is very important. Arrows point from one step to the next. Between steps a change occurs.

Some process diagrams are used to show how to make or do something. Often it is easier to demonstrate a task using a picture than it is to write step-by-step instructions. More often a picture or diagram is needed to make step-by-step instructions easier to understand.

Example The diagram below shows how to make a worm habitat, or wormery, from a shoebox. Wormeries can be used to study food chains.

This type of diagram usually has a list of materials needed for the task. The sizes of the parts are usually shown in true proportion to one another. For example, the layers of potting soil are much thicker than the layers of sand. Another way of saying this is that the diagram is "drawn to scale."

Content Clue

Earthworms live in warm, moist soil. They churn up the ground and make it more fertile as they eat decaying plant matter and soil.

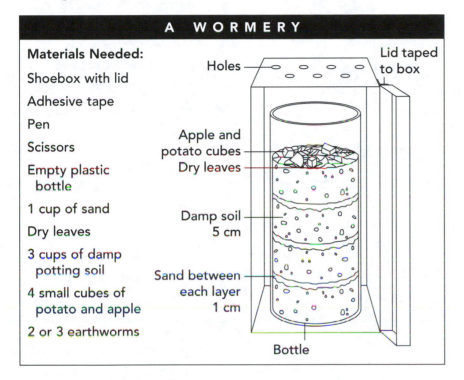

A WORMERY

Materials Needed:

Shoebox with lid

Adhesive tape

Pen

Scissors

Empty plastic bottle

1 cup of sand

Dry leaves

3 cups of damp potting soil

4 small cubes of potato and apple

2 or 3 earthworms

Holes

Lid taped to box

Apple and potato cubes

Dry leaves

Damp soil 5 cm

Sand between each layer 1 cm

Bottle

Do you think you could make a wormery by just using the materials list and diagram? _____
Based on the diagram, how do you think you would use a wormery? _____

A well-planned instruction diagram can replace most written instructions. This type of diagram is usually included with products that need to be assembled by the buyer.

Very often there will be no written instructions. Even the list of materials and the tools needed for assembly will be shown as pictures. A diagram like this one eliminates the need to include instructions in several different languages.

Test Tip

Assembly-instruction diagrams often use arrows to show the sequence of assembly.

Practice

Living and Nonliving Things

Base your answers to questions 1–4 on the diagram below, which compares an animal cell with a plant cell.

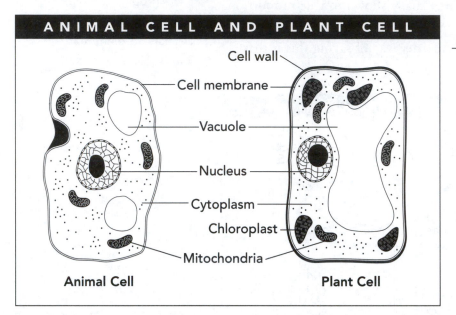

ANIMAL CELL AND PLANT CELL

Cell wall
Cell membrane
Vacuole
Nucleus
Cytoplasm
Chloroplast
Mitochondria

Animal Cell   Plant Cell

There are more similarities between plant and animal cells than there are differences.

Test Tip

Sometimes the drawings in a diagram share labels. A line may point to one or both illustrations. If it points to both, the two drawings have that same part in common.

1 Which cell part is present in the plant cell but not in the animal cell?

    1 vacuole   3 chloroplast

    2 cell membrane   4 nucleus

2 Which activity do plant cells perform that animal cells do not perform?

    1 respiration   3 reproduction

    2 photosynthesis   4 locomotion

3 Which cell part is larger in plant cells than in animal cells?

    1 cell membrane   3 cytoplasm

    2 vacuole   4 nucleus

4 What is the substance that surrounds the nucleus of the cell?

Content Clue

Remember that plants are **producers.** They use water, **carbon dioxide, chlorophyll,** and the **energy** in sunlight to make their own food.

Practice

Genetic Information

The chart below shows sickle-cell anemia being passed through several generations of a family. Base your answers to questions 1–5 on this chart.

📖 **Content Clue**

A **pedigree chart** is used to study inherited **diseases** or disorders. It is similar to a "family tree." Other inherited disorders include color blindness and hemophilia.

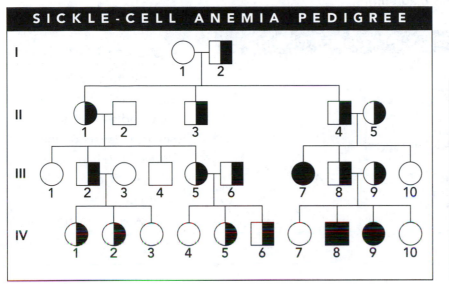

SICKLE-CELL ANEMIA PEDIGREE

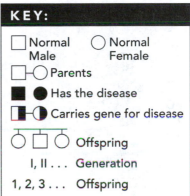

KEY:

☐ Normal Male   ○ Normal Female

☐—○ Parents

■ ● Has the disease

◨—◐ Carries gene for disease

○ ☐ ○ Offspring

I, II . . . Generation

1, 2, 3 . . . Offspring

1 How many generations are represented in this chart?

_____

_____

2 How many carriers of the sickle-cell trait are in each generation?

_____

3 How many people in the family were born with the disease of sickle-cell anemia?

_____

4 From which parent did the second-generation children inherit the sickle-cell gene?

_____

5 In which generation did sickle-cell anemia first actually appear?

_____

Practice

Change Over Time

The diagram below shows two undisturbed deposits of sedimentary rock that contain fossils. It also shows a fossil that might be found in a layer of this rock. Base your answers to questions 1–4 on this diagram.

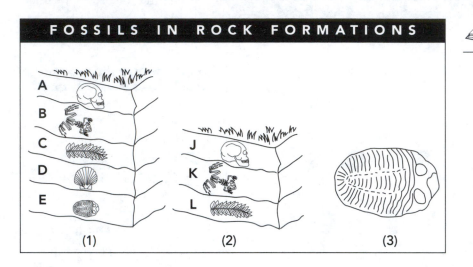

FOSSILS IN ROCK FORMATIONS

(1) (2) (3)

Content Clues

Sedimentary rock, like sandstone, is formed when sand and silt in water collect in layers on the bottom and harden over millions of years. Three-quarters of the Earth's surface is sedimentary rock.

1 In rock formation (1), which layer was deposited first? How do you know?

_____

_____

2 Read each statement below. Based on the diagram, which one is accurate?

   1 Fossils in Layer C are the same age as those in Layer L.

   2 Fossils in Layer B are the same age as those in Layer J.

   3 Fossils in Layer A were formed first.

   4 Fossils in Layer L are the same age as those in Layer E.

Content Clue

The remains of **organisms** trapped in sedimentary rock often form **fossils.**

3 Which layers in rock formation (1) match the layers in rock formation (2)?

   1 A, B, and C   3 C, D, and E

   2 B, C, and D   4 A, C, and D

4 On a separate sheet of paper, explain how the trilobite fossil (3) could be used to determine the age of the rock layers. Keep in mind that scientists know when trilobites lived.

Practice

Reproduction and Development

The diagram below shows the parts of a flower. Study the flower parts; then answer questions 1–6.

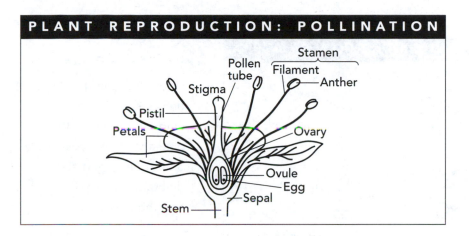

PLANT REPRODUCTION: POLLINATION

1 Which flower part is the male reproductive organ?

   1 pistil   3 stamen

   2 seed   4 ovary

2 How many stamens does this flower have?

_____

3 Which flower part is the female reproductive organ?

   1 pistil   3 stamen

   2 pollen   4 ovary

4 Many flowers are pollinated by insects. What role do the flower's petals have in that process?

_____

_____

_____

5 How many ovules does this flower have?

_____

6 Name the parts of the stamen.

_____

Content Clue

Pollen contains the male reproductive cell. It is produced in the anther.

Content Clue

The **ovule** in seed-bearing plants is the container for the **egg.**

Practice

Meeting Daily Needs

The diagram below shows the skulls of several different animals. Study the teeth of these animals to answer questions 1–4 below.

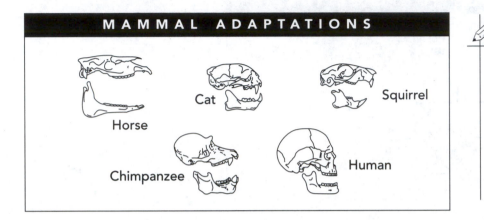

MAMMAL ADAPTATIONS

Horse

Cat

Squirrel

Chimpanzee

Human

✏️ **Test Tip**

Read all of the questions before studying the diagram. Knowing the questions helps you focus on the parts of the diagram where you will find the answers.

1 Which of the mammals shown have large canine teeth for tearing?

_____

2 How are the teeth in the diagram appropriate for each mammal's diet? Use two specific examples from the diagram as part of your explanation.

_____

_____

_____

_____

_____

3 Based on your answer to question 1 and what you already know, how would you classify humans?

    1 producers   3 omnivores

    2 herbivores   4 decomposers

4 All the mammals in the diagram are

    1 producers   3 omnivores

    2 consumers   4 decomposers

📖 **Content Clues**

Herbivores eat only plants. **Carnivores** eat only meat. **Omnivores** eat both plants and meat.

Practice

Energy in Ecosystems

A food web shows feeding relationships among the species in a community. Study the food web diagram below, then answer questions 1–3.

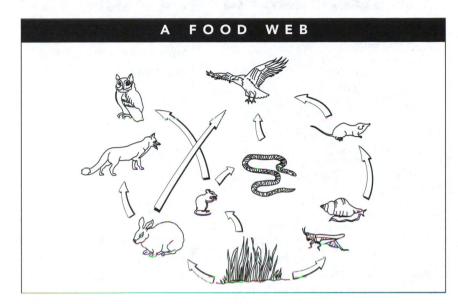

A FOOD WEB

Test Tip

The arrows in a **food web** diagram point toward the **consumers**.

1 Which of the following is a food chain within this food web?

    1 grasshopper → grass → rabbit

    2 snake → rabbit → hawk

    3 grass → mouse → owl

    4 mouse → hawk → snake

Content Clue

A food web is made up of many interconnected **food chains**.

2 In which direction is energy flowing through this food web? Give an example that uses four of the organisms shown.

    _____

    _____

3 Explain what would happen in this food web if the grass became polluted. Assume that the pollutant does not kill the grass immediately. Which organisms will accumulate the most pollutant in their bodies?

    _____

    _____

    _____

Practice

Humans and the Environment

Study the map and table to answer questions 1–4.

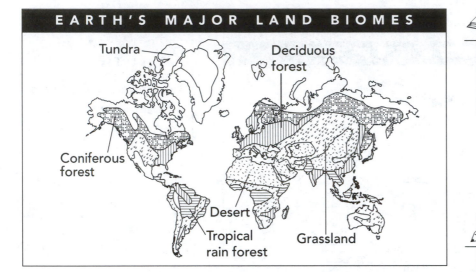

EARTH'S MAJOR LAND BIOMES

Tundra
Deciduous forest
Coniferous forest
Desert
Tropical rain forest
Grassland

Content Clue

Biomes are major regions with similar climates and plantlife.

Biome	Average Yearly Rainfall	Average Yearly Temperature Range
Tundra	less than 25 cm	−25°C–4°C
Coniferous Forest	25–75 cm	−10°C–14°C
Deciduous Forest	75–125 cm	6°C–28°C
Tropical Rain Forest	200–450 cm	25°C–28°C
Grassland	25–75 cm	0°C–25°C
Desert	less than 25 cm	24°C–40°C

Test Tip

Maps may use line patterns instead of colors to indicate different areas.

Test Tip

Diagrams are often accompanied by a chart that gives more information.

1 Which type of biome is found in the northeastern United States?

_____

2 Which type of biome is found in northern Africa? How much rain would you expect to fall yearly in this biome?

_____

3 Which biome receives the most yearly rainfall?

_____

4 Which biome has the highest average temperatures?

_____

Practice

The Earth and Space

Base your answers to questions 1–6 on the diagram below, which shows the solar system.

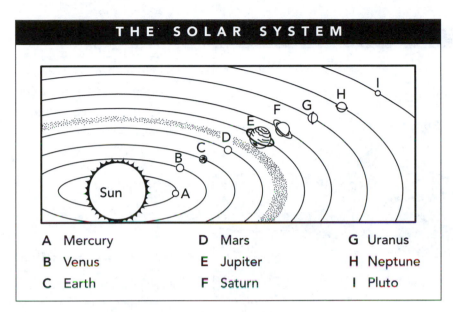

THE SOLAR SYSTEM

A Mercury	D Mars	G Uranus
B Venus	E Jupiter	H Neptune
C Earth	F Saturn	I Pluto

✏️ **Test Tip**

Some diagrams have a *key*, or *legend*. The key is a list of labels set to one side or below the diagram.

1 Which is the largest planet?

  1 Pluto   3 Jupiter

  2 Earth   4 Sun

2 What is the star in this solar system called?

  1 Venus   3 a comet

  2 the Sun   4 Earth

3 Which is the sixth planet from the Sun?

_____

4 Which letter in the legend indicates the planet Earth?

_____

5 Between which two planets is the asteroid belt found?

_____

6 Which object contains most of the matter in the solar system?

  1 Jupiter   3 Earth

  2 Mars   4 the Sun

Content Clues

Use this to remember the order of the planets: "My Very Enchanting Mother Just Served Us Nine Pizzas." The first letter of each word stands for a planet. For example, the **M** in **M**y stands for Mercury.

The **asteroid** belt contains many thousands of rocklike objects that vary in size.

Practice

The Interaction of Air, Land, and Water

Base your answers to questions 1–4 on the diagram below, which shows the water cycle.

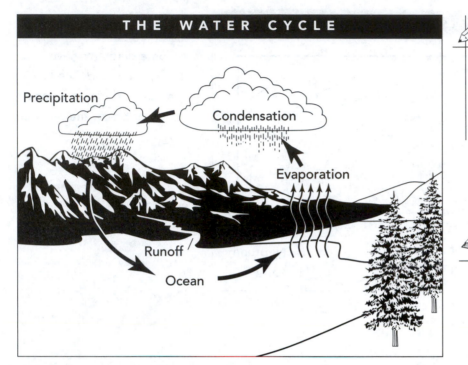

THE WATER CYCLE

Precipitation

Condensation

Evaporation

Runoff

Ocean

Water moves continuously between the atmosphere and the surface of the Earth.

Test Tip

Follow the arrows in a diagram to understand the order of the steps in the process being shown.

Content Clue

Evaporation is caused by heat energy from the Sun.

1 As ocean water evaporates, it

    1 falls as rain   **3** forms a river

    2 rises   **4** moves toward the mountains

2 Clouds form by the process of

    1 evaporation   **3** condensation

    2 the ocean   **4** rain

3 What happens in the water cycle after water vapor rises?

_____

_____

4 Explain the movement of water in the water cycle.

_____

_____

Test Tip

For a "short answer" question, if you are not sure how much to write, write at least one full sentence. Start your sentence by using part of the question in your answer. This is called "echoing the question."

Practice

Physical Properties of Matter

Base your answers to questions 1–5 on the diagram of the carbon atom shown below.

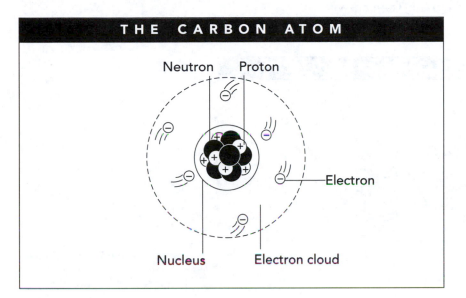

THE CARBON ATOM

1 How many electrons does this atom have?

_____

2 What is carbon's atomic number? How can you tell?

_____

Content Clue

Atomic number is the number of **protons** in an **atom**.

3 How many other elements have the same atomic number as carbon? Explain your answer.

_____

_____

_____

Content Clue

The **atomic mass** number is the total number of protons and **neutrons** in an atom.

4 What is the mass number of carbon?

_____

5 Compare the number of protons to the number of electrons in this atom. Is this atom neutral? Explain your answer.

_____

_____

Practice

Forms of Energy

The diagram below shows an electrical circuit, which is made up of a battery, a switch, two bulbs, and the wire connecting them. Study the diagram. Then answer questions 1–5 below.

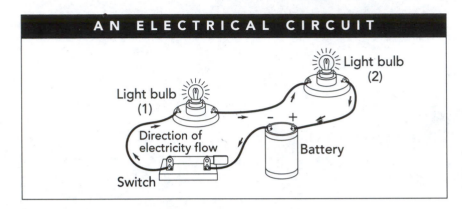

1 Is this a series circuit or a parallel circuit?

_____

2 If bulb (1) were to go out, bulb (2) would
  1 be brighter
  2 be dimmer
  3 remain the same
  4 go out

3 What would happen if you added a third bulb to this circuit?
  1 All the bulbs would give off less light.
  2 The circuit would overload and burn out.
  3 The battery would die.
  4 The circuit would be one-third brighter.

4 In which direction is the current flowing in this circuit?

_____

_____

_____

5 What would happen to the bulbs if the switch were opened?

_____

Content Clue

In a **series circuit**, the current flows through the components one after the other. In a **parallel circuit**, the current passes through all the parts at once.

Content Clue

In a simple **circuit** such as this one, **electrical energy** is converted to **heat** and **light energy**.

Practice

Forces and Motion

The diagram below shows a magnet and the magnet's magnetic field. Study the diagram. Then answer questions 1–5.

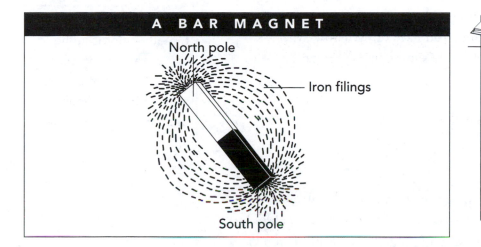

A BAR MAGNET

North pole

Iron filings

South pole

Content Clue

Iron filings are often scattered around a **magnet** so that the **magnetic field** can be seen. Diagrams of magnetic fields show the pattern produced by the iron filings.

1 What do the iron filings around this magnet show?

_____

2 A compass needle is a magnet that points to the Earth's North and South poles. How could you use a compass to find what direction you are facing?

_____

_____

3 Where near the magnet would you find the most lines of force?

_____

4 Where is the magnetic field the strongest?

_____

5 How could a wire and this magnet be used to produce an electric current?

_____

_____

_____

CHAPTER 4

Improving Reading and Writing Skills

Reading Strategies

Tests sometimes contain words that are unfamiliar or reading passages that are difficult to understand. During most tests you won't have a dictionary at hand. You have to figure out what the words mean on your own. Here are some things you can do:

- use context clues

- find key words in a passage

- state the main idea

Use Context Clues

The way a word is used in a sentence and the words surrounding it make up the word's context. The word *context* comes from an old English word that means "the weaving together of words." You can use a sentence's context to help you determine the meaning of unfamiliar words.

Example Sometimes a word is defined directly, as in the following passage.

> Xylem is a type of plant tissue. It transports water and minerals from the roots of the plant to the rest of the plant. It also supports the plant.

The first sentence defines the word *xylem,* and the next two sentences give more details that make the meaning clearer.

Some passages contain only general, or indirect, clues about the meaning of a word.

Example Read the following passage and see if you can guess at the meanings of the words *unicellular* and *multicellular.*

> One way organisms change is by growing, or becoming larger. In a unicellular organism, growth occurs as new materials are added to the cell. The cells of a multicellular organism also grow, as new material is added to each cell. However, most growth in multicellular organisms is caused by the formation of new cells.

Note that the sentence about the unicellular organism uses the singular form of the word *cell.* The text referring to the growth of a multicellular organism uses the plural form, *cells.* These are indirect clues that unicellular refers to one cell while multicellular refers to many cells.

Test Tip

When a word is defined by the other words in the sentence, the sentence will contain a linking verb. One such verb is *is.* Verbs like *appear* or *seem* are also linking verbs.

Content Clue

Phloem is another kind of plant **tissue. Xylem** and phloem together make up a plant's vascular system. These networks of tubes, or vessels, carry fluid and **nutrients** around the plant.

Content Clue

Two **kingdoms** consist mostly of **unicellular organisms,** the **Monera** and **Protist** kingdoms.

Find Key Words in a Passage

A key word is any word that can help you summarize the content of a passage. Key words may be the subjects of sentences or actions described. You identify key words to help you organize in your mind the information you read.

Example Try to identify the key words in the following paragraph. The first two are *sound* and *vibrate*.

> Sound is caused by objects that vibrate. These vibrations move the air around them to form sound waves. The frequency of the vibration determines the pitch of the sound that is produced. The amplitude of the vibration determines the loudness of the sound.

The key words in this paragraph include _____

_____

On tests you are sometimes asked to read a passage and then answer questions about it. Finding key words can help you answer these questions. Suppose on a test you were told to read the paragraph above, then to answer the following question:

> How can you change the pitch of a sound?

First, identify the key words in the question. _____

_____

Next, skim the paragraph and find these same words in the selection. This will help you locate the sentence that contains the information you need to answer the question. Now you can answer the question.

State the Main Idea

A passage can be summarized in one statement, called the main idea. Figuring out the main idea of a passage can help you understand what the whole passage is about. Often the main idea is stated directly in the first or last sentence of the paragraph. When it is not stated directly in the paragraph, you need to state it in your own words. Reread the paragraph above about sound. What is the main idea? _____

_____

Where is it stated in the passage? _____

_____

Test Tip

Key words can also be little words such as *not*, *all*, and *none*. These are especially important to note in the questions you are being asked.

Content Clue

Frequency is the number of waves that pass a given point each second.

Test Tips

Most tests don't give you much time. Practice these reading skills before your test, until you can do them quickly and easily.

Another way to be sure you understand a passage is to restate it in your own words. First, read the passage. Then, identify key words and the main idea. Finally, put it all in your own words.

Writing Strategies

Most tests include some questions that ask you to write out the answers rather than choose one from a list. Some of these questions can be answered in one or two words, some require one or two sentences, and some require one or several paragraphs. In all cases, you need to pay attention to spelling, punctuation, grammar, and organization of thoughts. This helps the teacher understand what you are trying to say. It will also help *you* understand what you are trying to say.

Short-Answer Questions

Answers That Require Less Than a Sentence These questions resemble completion questions. The answers need to be brief. Sometimes one word will answer the question. Other times a sentence fragment is enough.

Example Suppose you were given the following question:

> Heat moves by conduction, convection, and radiation. A pan of water is sitting on a hot stove. Which method does heat use to travel from the stove to the pan?

First analyze the question. Exactly what are you being asked? Note that you are *not* being asked to describe how the water is heated, only how the stove heats the pan. The best answer here is one word only: *conduction.*

One- or Two-Sentence Answers These answers should be clear and to the point.

Example Suppose you were given the following question:

> Name the inner planets in our solar system and describe the differences between these planets and the outer planets.

This question has several parts. The first part asks you to name the inner planets. The second part asks you to describe the differences between the two groups. A good answer would be:

The inner planets are Mercury, Venus, Earth, and Mars. The inner planets are all small and rocky. Except for Pluto, the outer planets are large and made mostly of gas. Pluto is small and dense.

Test Tip

If the question asks you to describe or explain something, write at least several sentences, even if the question does not tell you how much to write.

Content Clue

Conduction is the transfer of **heat** by **molecules** of **matter** bumping into one another. **Convection** is the transfer of heat within a liquid or gas by the movement of warmer particles. **Radiation** is the transfer of **energy** by **electromagnetic** waves.

Test Tip

Always make sure you answer both parts to a two-part question.

Paragraphs

Some questions require fairly long responses, or full paragraphs. These answers need to be well thought out and carefully written. Sometimes these types of answers are marked wrong on tests because they are so disorganized the teacher can't tell what is being described. As you write, make sure your ideas flow in a logical order and lead the reader to your conclusions.

To help you write paragraphs, follow these steps:

1. Analyze the question.

2. Brainstorm.

3. Make an outline or rough draft.

4. Write out your answer.

5. Read over your answer and make corrections.

Example Suppose you were given the following question:

How do sexual reproduction, mutation, and changes in the environment work together to cause changes in species over time?

1. Analyze the Question What is the question asking? It's asking how a species changes over time. It doesn't ask about variations among individuals but about long-term changes in species. Make sure this is the question you answer.

2. Brainstorm Make a list of everything you can think of that might be useful in answering the question. Don't limit yourself here. You can weed out unnecessary information later. Here are some ideas you might include in your list for this question:

- evolution
- genetics
- DNA
- variation
- change in climate

- chromosomes
- meiosis
- geographic isolation
- competition from new species

 **Test Tip**

Brainstorm means to write down thoughts about a particular topic as they pop into your head.

Content Clues

Evolution refers to gradual change. When something evolves, it usually changes slowly.

A **mutation** is a sudden genetic change. It can be caused by something in the **environment,** such as chemicals or **radiation.**

3. Make an Outline or a Rough Draft Organize the information from your list. Next, write an outline of the main ideas you plan to cover in your answer or write a rough draft.

After each main idea in the outline or rough draft, make a list of points to include in your answer. The outline or rough draft will help you decide the order in which information should be presented. It will also help you spot any missing information and eliminate those things on your list that are not useful. Here is a possible outline for the changes in species question:

Species Change Over Time

I. *The mixing together of chromosomes during sexual reproduction (meiosis) causes variation in offspring.*

II. *Mutations in DNA can cause variations in individuals that are passed down to offspring.*

III. *When environmental conditions change, only certain individuals, ones who have beneficial traits due to genetic variation, survive.*

IV. *These work together to cause species to change.*

    A. *The variations caused by sexual reproduction and mutations produce some individuals with traits that enable them to better survive in the new environment.*

    B. *Many of the individuals with the beneficial traits survive and pass these traits on to their offspring. Fewer of the individuals without the beneficial traits survive to pass on their traits to their offspring.*

    C. *Over time, the number of individuals with the beneficial traits increases while the number of individuals without them declines.*

Content Clue

In **sexual reproduction**, one set of **chromosomes** comes from the male. The other set comes from the female.

Review the outline. Note that it is simple and logical. It follows a reasonable sequence. It does not include information that is not needed. Finally, it answers the question.

4. Write Out Your Answer Using the information in your outline or rough draft, write out the answer to the question. A possible answer to the question might be:

The mixing together of chromosomes during sexual reproduction causes variation in individual offspring. Mutations in DNA can also cause variation in individuals. If an environment changes, the traits individuals need to survive may also change. The variation caused by sexual reproduction and mutations mean that some individuals are born with traits that may let them survive better in the new environment. Individuals with traits that let them survive are more likely to pass on these traits to their offspring. Individuals without the traits that let them survive do not live long enough to pass on their traits to offspring. Over time, the number of individuals with the "survival" traits increases. The number of individuals without them decreases. This changes the species.

✎ **Test Tip**

In your answer you will probably be able to use phrases and sentences directly from your outline.

5. Read Over Your Answer and Make Corrections Always take a few moments to read over your answer, checking for mistakes. Things to check for include the following:

- Your ideas flow logically and lead to a conclusion.

- The answer gives enough details to make your ideas clear. It also sticks to the point and does not confuse the reader with unneeded information.

- Words are spelled correctly.

- Each sentence begins with a capital letter and ends with a period or other closing punctuation mark.

- Each sentence has a subject and a verb and the subjects and verbs agree.

- Verb forms are correct and tenses used are logical.

- There are no run-on sentences or sentence fragments.

- Antecedents to pronouns such as *it* or *this* are clear.

- Adjectives are not being used as adverbs and vice versa (good vs. well).

Practice

Living and Nonliving Things

For questions 1–3, write your answers in the space provided. Base your answer to question 1 on the information below and on your knowledge of science.

> Monerans and protists are one-celled organisms. Monerans include such simple organisms as bacteria and cyanobacteria, or blue-green bacteria. More complex one-celled organisms, such as amoebas, paramecia, and diatoms, are protists. Protists have membrane-bound organelles such as food vacuoles and nuclei. Monerans have no membrane-bound organelles. Instead, the DNA and other materials a moneran needs to carry on its life processes float in the cell's cytoplasm.

 **Test Tip**

Make a two-column chart of the information in this paragraph. Put all the information about **monerans** in one column. Put all the information about **protists** in the other.

1 Compare and contrast protists and monerans. Give one difference and one similarity.

_____

_____

_____

2 Name two differences between bacteria and viruses.

_____

_____

_____

Content Clue

Viruses are not in any **kingdom** because many scientists do not consider them living things.

3 Describe the relationship between a tissue, an organ, and a system.

_____

_____

_____

4 On a separate sheet of paper, describe how the respiratory and circulatory systems work together to provide cells with oxygen and remove carbon dioxide.

Content Clue

The **respiratory system** includes the lungs. The **circulatory system** includes the heart and **blood vessels**.

Practice

Genetic Information

For questions 1–4, write your answers in the space provided.

1 Two daughter skin cells have just been formed as a result of mitosis. What do you know about their chromosomes?

_____

_____

_____

2 Describe the relationship between DNA, chromosomes, and genes.

_____

_____

_____

3 Barbara Jacob has detached earlobes. The gene for detached earlobes is dominant. Her husband, Jason, has attached earlobes. The gene for attached earlobes is recessive. What pairs of genes for earlobes could Barbara have? What pairs of genes for earlobes could Jason have?

_____

_____

_____

4 Complete the Punnett squares below to show how the Jacobs' genes for earlobes will be passed on to their children. Use "E" for the gene for detached earlobes and "e" for the gene for attached lobes. On a separate sheet of paper, explain how to interpret the resulting Punnett squares.

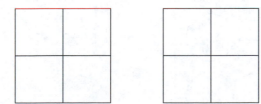

Content Clues

Mitosis is very similar to **asexual reproduction** in **organisms.**

A **DNA molecule** looks like a twisted ladder. It is sometimes called a "double helix."

Content Clue

Genes mostly occur in pairs. They are either both dominant, both recessive, or a combination of dominant and recessive. In a **Punnett square,** a dominant gene is represented by a capital letter. A recessive gene is represented by a lowercase letter.

Practice

Change Over Time

For questions 1 and 2, write your answers in the space provided. Base your answer to question 1 on the information below and on your knowledge of science.

A population of rabbits lived on an island. A farmer introduced coyotes to the island. Because they lived on an island, the rabbits could not escape to a new area to live. Some of the rabbits that were faster because of genetic variations in running ability outran the coyotes. These rabbits passed down their ability to run fast to their offspring. Many of the slower rabbits were caught by the coyotes and therefore had no offspring.

1 Describe what eventually happened to the species of rabbits on this island.

_____

_____

_____

2 How do bees contribute to variations in plants?

_____

_____

_____

3 On a separate sheet of paper, explain how the process of meiosis leads to variations in members of a species.

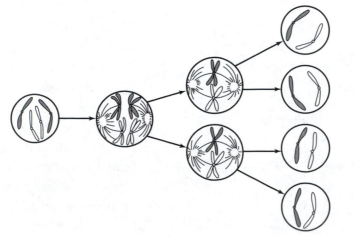

Content Clue

Introduced means to "bring a new **species** to a place where that species has never been before." Introduced species can cause **extinctions** and upset the balance of an **ecosystem**.

Content Clues

Plants can be pollinated by wind, bats, and insects.

In **asexual reproduction**, the **chromosomes** in all daughter **cells** are usually identical to the chromosomes in the parent cell.

Test Tip

To better understand a question, restate it in your own words.

Practice

Reproduction and Development

For questions 1 and 2, write your answers in the space provided. Base your answer to question 1 on the information below and on your knowledge of science.

Ferns are simple vascular plants that reproduce by a process called alternation of generations. In one generation a fern plant, called a sporophyte, produces asexual reproductive cells called spores. Each spore grows to form a small heart-shaped plant called a gametophyte. In the next generation, the gametophyte produces male and female sex cells called gametes. These cells unite to form a fertilized egg, which grows into a fern plant.

1 In alternation of generations, the plant that produces sexual reproductive cells is called a prothallus. Which generation in the passage above is the prothallus?

_____

_____

_____

2 In multicellular organisms such as plants and animals, which cells are produced by meiosis?

_____

_____

_____

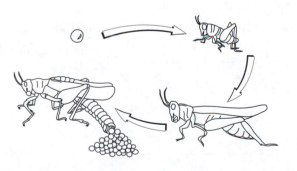

3 Look at the diagram of the life cycle of a grasshopper. On a separate sheet of paper, describe the stages and compare its life cycle to the life cycle of a butterfly.

> **✏ Test Tip**
>
> Find the key words in the question. They will help you find the answer.

> **📖 Content Clue**
>
> There are two types of **metamorphosis**, complete and incomplete.

Practice

Meeting Daily Needs

For questions 1–4, write your answers in the space provided.
Base your answer to question 1 on the information below
and on your knowledge of science.

Humans and other animals obtain energy from carbohydrates
and fats in the foods they eat. Some examples of carbohydrates
are bread, rice, and potatoes. Fats are found in oils, nuts, milk,
and many high-calorie nutrient-deficient foods. Energy is
released from carbohydrates and fats when they are broken
down inside animals' body cells.

1 What provides an animal with the energy it needs?

_____

2 How do mammals maintain their body temperatures?

_____

_____

_____

Content Clue

Mammals are **warm-
blooded.** They rely on the
process of **metabolism** to
get **energy** that can be
used for various purposes.

3 How are the gills of a fish and the lungs of a human similar?

_____

_____

_____

4 Name two ways your body keeps viruses from infecting you.
Then describe two ways your body can restore itself to a healthy
state after a viral infection. Use additional paper if you need to.

_____

_____

_____

_____

Content Clue

The body **system** that
responds to **viruses** is
the **immune system.**

Practice

Energy in Ecosystems

For questions 1–3, write your answers in the space provided. Base your answer to question 1 on the information below and on your knowledge of science. Base your answers to questions 2 and 3 on the diagram.

Carbon dioxide and oxygen flow through ecosystems in a cycle called the carbon dioxide-oxygen cycle. This cycle includes the processes of photosynthesis, in which plants take in carbon dioxide and give off oxygen, and respiration, in which all organisms take in oxygen and give off carbon dioxide. These processes help keep the balance of carbon dioxide and oxygen in the atmosphere fairly constant.

Test Tip

Draw a diagram of the **cycle** described. Then restate the question as a statement with the answer at the end.

1 Do plants take in more carbon dioxide during the day or at night? Why?

_____

_____

_____

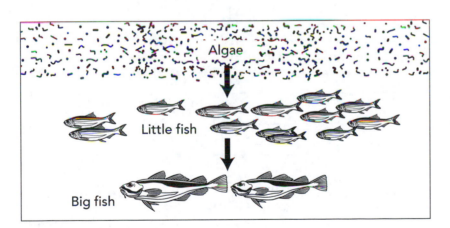

2 Name the producer in this food chain.

_____

3 Which organism in the food chain is a secondary consumer?

_____

Content Clue

The flow of **energy** through an **ecosystem** can be shown in a diagram of a **food chain**.

4 Julia ate a piece of chicken. The energy she got from the chicken originally came from the Sun. On a separate sheet of paper, describe how the energy moved from the Sun to Julia.

Practice

Humans and the Environment

For questions 1–3, write your answers in the space provided. Base your answers to questions 1 and 2 on the information below and on your knowledge of science.

There are different forms of symbiosis, or relationships between organisms. Some of these are parasitism, commensalism, and mutualism. In parasitism, one organism benefits while the other is harmed. In commensalism, one organism benefits while the other is neither helped nor harmed. In mutualism, both organisms benefit. Clownfish protect themselves from predators by living among the poisonous tentacles of sea anemones. The clownfish have a covering of mucus that protects them from the poison in the tentacles. The sea anemones feed on bits of food dropped by the clownfish.

1 Name the type of relationship between clownfish and sea anemones.

_____

_____

2 What is the difference between mutualism and commensalism?

_____

_____

_____

3 Describe the relationship between natural resources and conservation.

_____

_____

_____

4 In the science of ecology, the terms *population* and *community* have special meanings. On a separate sheet of paper, tell how an ecologist would describe the relationship between a population, a community, and an ecosystem. Give an example of each.

✏ **Test Tip**

Underline the key words in the paragraph. Use context clues to help you understand the meanings of the terms and find the answers to the questions.

📖 **Content Clue**

Some important **natural resources** to humans are **fossil fuels**, **minerals** such as **metals**, and water.

✏ **Test Tip**

Start by defining the terms **population, community,** and **ecosystem.**

Practice

The Earth and Space

For questions 1–3, write your answers in the space provided. Base your answer to question 1 on the information below and on your knowledge of science.

Saturn isn't the only planet with rings. The other gas giants—Jupiter, Uranus, and Neptune—also have rings. However, they are much thinner and harder to see than Saturn's rings. The rings are made up of rocky or icy pieces of matter between about 1 centimeter and 2 meters in diameter. The gaps between some of the rings are probably caused by gravitational interactions between the planets and their moons.

1 Which planets do not have rings?

_____

2 The tilt of the Earth's axis causes longer, warmer days in summer. What happens in winter because of the tilt? Why?

_____

_____

Sun

Moon

Earth

3 This diagram shows the positions of the Earth, Moon, and Sun. On a separate sheet of paper, name the phase of the Moon and describe how it looks in the sky.

4 The Earth is at perihelion during the month of January. On a separate sheet of paper, explain why January is not the warmest month of the year in the Northern Hemisphere.

✏️ **Test Tip**

Note any key words in the question such as *not, all,* or *none.*

📖 **Content Clue**

Differences in **temperature** and day length over a year depend on how much of the Sun's **energy** strikes the Earth's surface.

📖 **Content Clue**

Perihelion is the point in an **orbit** of a planet or other body when that body is closest to the Sun.

Practice

The Interaction of Air, Land, and Water

For questions 1 and 2, write your answers in the space provided. Base your answers to questions 1 and 2 on the information below and on your knowledge of science.

Water responds more slowly to changes in temperature than does land. On the seacoast, once the Sun comes up, the land warms up faster than the ocean. The air over the land also warms up faster than the air over the water. The cool air over the ocean moves in and pushes up the warmer air over the land. This is called a sea breeze. At night the opposite happens. The land cools down faster than the ocean, and the cool air over the land moves out and pushes up the warmer air over the ocean. This is a land breeze.

✏️ **Test Tip**

To help you understand the processes described here, make a rough sketch with arrows showing the movement of air.

1 When does a sea breeze form?

_____

_____

_____

2 What causes a land breeze?

_____

_____

_____

Base your answers to questions 3 and 4 on the information below and on your knowledge of science.

Wind is moving air. Heat causes the molecules in all matter to move. The warmer the air is, the more its molecules spread out. In other words, it becomes less dense. Air that is less dense rises. Cold, dense air sweeps into the empty space left by the warmer air. This sets up a motion of air called a convection current.

📖 **Content Clue**

The source of almost all **energy** on the Earth is the Sun.

3 What is the source of the energy that drives the convection current?

_____

4 On a separate sheet of paper, describe how convection currents form large wind systems.

Practice

Physical Properties of Matter

For questions 1 and 2, write your answers in the space provided.

1 The illustrations below show an inflated balloon and a glass marble, each on a balance scale. List three physical properties of the marble and three properties of the balloon.

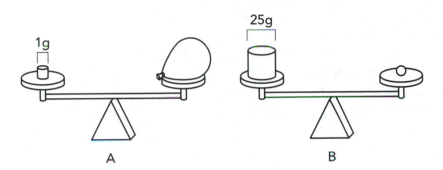

A   B

> **Content Clue**
>
> Physical properties are sometimes called characteristics. Some physical properties are color, odor, **mass,** volume, **density, solubility,** and ability to conduct **heat** or **electricity,** among other things.

_____

_____

_____

2 Jerry spilled sugar and iron filings into a pile of sand. How can Jerry separate these three substances from each other?

_____

_____

_____

> **Content Clue**
>
> Some substances are **soluble** (dissolve) in water. Some **metals** are magnetic.

3 On a separate sheet of paper, describe the difference between a physical change and a chemical change.

4 On Friday John left an ice cube in a glass near a warm, sunny window. When he went back on Monday, he found the glass completely empty. John knew that no one had been in the room over the weekend. On a separate sheet of paper, describe what happened to the molecules in the ice cube that had been in the glass.

Practice

Forms of Energy

**For question 1, write your answer in the space provided.
Base your answer to question 1 on the information below
and on your knowledge of science.**

> Sound is caused by vibrating objects, which move the air
> around them to form sound waves. On a violin, the initial
> vibration is caused by the force of the bow moving across a
> string. The body of the violin then resonates with the string's
> vibrations and makes them stronger. The violinist puts a finger
> on the string to change the pitch. The shorter a given string,
> the faster it vibrates when the bow moves across it. This makes
> the pitch it produces higher. To play a louder sound, the
> violinist transfers more energy through the bow to the string,
> thus increasing the amplitude of the moving string and of the
> sound waves it produces.

1 Why does changing the length of a violin string change its pitch?

_____

_____

_____

Test Tip

Identify the key words
in the question and then
locate those words in the
paragraph. This will help
you quickly find the
information you need
to answer the question.

2 The temperature shown on a mercury thermometer was 25°C.
John put the thermometer in a glass of warm water and it
changed to show a temperature of 35°C. On a separate sheet of
paper, explain what happened to the molecules of mercury in the
thermometer when it was put in warm water.

Content Clue

Heat makes **molecules**
move faster and spread
apart.

Practice

Forces and Motion

For questions 1–3, write your answers in the space provided.
Base your answer to question 1 on the information below
and on your knowledge of science.

Friction is a force that opposes motion. When two pieces
of matter move past each other, friction slows both of them
down. Friction is a result of interactions between the atoms
on the surfaces of the pieces of matter. These atoms form
bonds between the two surfaces, and the bonds have to be
broken in order for the matter to move.

Test Tip

Pick out the key words in
this passage and the main
idea. Then restate the
passage in your own
words.

1 What part do atoms play in friction?

_____

_____

_____

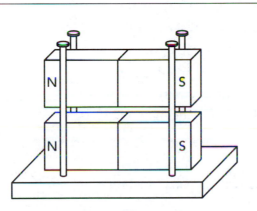

Content Clue

Magnetic poles are the
parts of **magnetic fields**
where the **magnetism** is
concentrated. Unlike poles
attract each other. Like
poles repel each other.

2 Look at the diagram above. What will happen if the top magnet
is rotated so that its end marked *N* is over the end marked *S* on
the bottom magnet?

_____

_____

_____

3 The amount of gravitational pull an object exerts depends
on what?

_____

_____

CHAPTER 5

Science Inquiry Skills

Scientists use special inquiry skills to answer questions, gather information, and do experiments. You will need to apply similar skills such as the following, as you take the Grade 8 Intermediate-Level Science Test:

- Hypothesizing
- Predicting
- Observing
- Measuring

- Analyzing
- Inferring
- Comparing and Contrasting
- Classifying

- Modeling
- Recognizing Cause and Effect
- Telling Fact from Opinion

Hypothesizing

When you state a hypothesis, you suggest an answer to a problem, based on what you already know. You can also think of a hypothesis as a possible explanation for why something occurs. You can support or reject a hypothesis by observing or experimenting. If your observations or experiments do not support your hypothesis, then you need to state a new hypothesis based on your discoveries. Stating a hypothesis is an important part of the scientific method.

Predicting

When you predict, you state what you think will happen, based on what you already know or have observed.

Example Astronomers know that the Earth, the other planets, and the Moon move in regular and predictable ways. They can use this knowledge to make accurate predictions. They can tell when lunar and solar eclipses will occur and when and where the planets will appear in the night sky.

If you make careful observations and measure and record what you observe, you can use that information to predict.

Observing

When you observe, you use all your senses. You must pay close attention to everything that happens. Often, you need to record your observations. What you see, hear, smell, touch, and taste can be important clues to figuring out what is going on.

Content Clue

Eclipses can be total or partial. Because of the angle of the Moon's **orbit** around the Earth, no more than seven eclipses (lunar and solar combined) can occur in one year.

Content Clue

Observing is part of the **scientific method.** The scientific method is a step-by-step procedure scientists use to do **experiments** and make discoveries.

Measuring

When you measure, you compare an unknown value with a known value, using units such as a gram or a millimeter. Measuring makes observations more exact and gives you a means of recording your results when you do an experiment.

Part of the Grade 8 Intermediate-Level Science Test will require you to perform an experiment that has already been set up for you. As part of the experiment, you may be asked to measure something and record the information on a chart.

Example You are asked to measure the temperature and the volume of ice water in a beaker. What unit of measurement would you use for temperature? _____ What unit would you use for volume? _____

Suppose the experiment calls for heating the water and measuring its temperature once every minute. What might be a good way to record these measurements? _____

By measuring how much the temperature changes over time, you are making a new measurement—the rate of temperature change.

Analyzing

After you record your observations and measurements in a table or chart, you can study the chart or table carefully, or analyze it.

Example Suppose you wanted to compare how quickly a truck and a car could stop on a road (stopping distances). After observing and making measurements, you could organize the information into the following table.

Stopping Distances on Dry Roads		
Speed	**Car**	**Truck**
60 kilometers per hour	40 meters	61 meters
80 kilometers per hour	74 meters	131 meters
100 kilometers per hour	111 meters	203 meters

After you have analyzed this information, you can use it to make a prediction. For example, if a truck at 60 kilometers per hour needs 61 meters to stop and a car needs only 40 meters, what can you predict about a truck that is following less than 21 meters behind the car? _____

_____

_____

Inferring

When you infer, you use logic and reasoning to form a statement that can be tested by an experiment or supported by evidence. This statement is based on known facts and observations.

Example Suppose you are an archaeologist, and you find the following objects buried at a prehistoric site: a spear, a stone ax head, a bone needle, a bone fishhook, and a stone knife blade. What can you infer about the people who left the objects behind? What activities did they do? _____

_____

_____

Content Clue

Before the **technology** of working with **metals** had been developed, people used bone, wood, and stone to make their tools.

Your inference should have been based on the knowledge that spears are usually used for hunting and fishhooks for fishing. What do you think people did with the bone needle? _____

Comparing and Contrasting

When you compare, you observe the characteristics of several things or events to see how they are alike (comparing) or different (contrasting). In the example above, the prehistoric items can be compared to similar objects used today. The bone needle is similar to needles used for sewing today. Therefore, you can infer that it was used for a similar purpose in prehistoric times.

Classifying

When you classify, you group things together based on how they are alike. People classify many different things, such as books in a library, groceries at a supermarket, or clothes in a closet. When given several objects, most people tend to sort them by similarities without even thinking about it.

Example Look at the illustration that follows. It shows a number of different organisms that can be classified in many different ways. One example might be into kingdoms—plant and animal. Name at least two other ways you could classify these organisms. _____

_____

Content Clue

Biologists classify **organisms** by their characteristics. One of those characteristics is the way the organism gets its food. Most of the organisms shown here get their food in the same way. They are **consumers.**

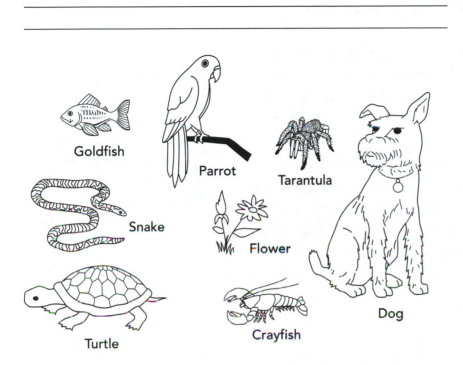

Goldfish

Parrot

Tarantula

Snake

Flower

Dog

Turtle

Crayfish

Classification makes the study of large groups or events less complex. In earth science, for example, rocks are classified into categories by how they were formed. If you find an igneous rock formation, you can assume it formed from molten rock. This, in turn, may mean that it came from a volcano.

Content Clue

Although **igneous rock** always forms from molten rock, it does not always come from the **lava** seeping out of a **volcano**. It may also form from **magma** inside the Earth.

Modeling

When you model, you use a visual representation of what you are studying to help explain it. A model can be a three-dimensional object, a drawing or blueprint, or a diagram. The model can be larger or smaller than the original. Modeling is especially useful when the object or event you are studying is too small or too large to study under normal conditions.

Example It is very hard to see an atom, even with a microscope. However, scientists have learned a lot about the structure of atoms from experiments. They can use what they have discovered to make models of atoms and molecules. They can use these models to form and test new hypotheses.

Recognizing Cause and Effect

A *cause* is what makes something happen. The *effect* is what happens. In science, you must be very careful in determining the actual cause of an effect. For example, just because you observe that it rained the night after a full Moon does not mean a full Moon causes rain.

In experimentation, cause and effect can be determined by controlling variables. A variable is anything that can influence the results of an experiment. A well-designed experiment tests only one variable at a time. That way, the true cause of an effect can be determined.

Example The drinking glasses from your dishwasher look cloudy. The repair technician who comes to your house has a hypothesis that there are two possible causes: either the water is not hot enough, or the new detergent you bought is not cleaning properly. How could you experiment to find out which one is the actual cause of the effect?_____

_____

_____

_____

_____

_____

If neither the water temperature nor the detergent turns out to be the cause, then the technician needs to form a new hypothesis.

Telling Fact from Opinion

A *fact* is a statement that can be proven true. An *opinion* is a statement of how someone feels or thinks about something. An opinion cannot be proven. Sometimes it is not easy to tell fact from opinion. The following steps may help you tell the difference.

1. Look for words such as *I believe* or *I think.* If something is a fact, the writer or speaker will not need to use these phrases.

2. Look for descriptive words or phrases that strongly suggest the positive or negative. For example, to say that gold is a yellow metal is to state a fact. To say that gold is a *beautiful* yellow metal is to state an opinion.

3. Ask yourself whether the statement can be proven by observing or testing. If it can, the statement is a fact.

✏️ **Test Tip**

You may not be asked directly about cause and effect on the examination. However, you will need to understand how it works in order to identify and work with **variables.**

Practice

Living and Nonliving Things

Base your answers to questions 1–4 on the passage below, which describes the kingdoms of life.

The kingdom Monera includes one-celled organisms, called monerans, that lack a nucleus. Bacteria make up this kingdom. The kingdom Protista contains organisms, called protists, that are also one-celled. However, these organisms have nuclei. Examples of protists include paramecia, amoebas, and some algae.

The kingdom Fungi contains both single-celled and many-celled organisms. These organisms have cell walls. Examples of fungi include molds, yeasts, and mushrooms. The kingdom Plantae consists of organisms with more than one cell, cell walls, and chlorophyll. Plants use chlorophyll during photosynthesis to make food. Examples of plants are mosses, ferns, and seed plants.

The kingdom Animalia also contains organisms with more than one cell. However, unlike plant cells, animal cells do not contain chlorophyll. Therefore, animals cannot make their own food. Animals must eat other organisms to survive. Insects, fish, reptiles, birds, and mammals are animals.

1 What is the term used to describe the major classification groups of organisms? _____

2 How many major classification groups of organisms are there?

_____

3 Compare and contrast the protist and the moneran classification groups. How are they alike and how are they different?

_____

_____

_____

4 Based on the passage, what can you infer about fish and reptiles?

_____

Content Clue

The first **organisms** on Earth most probably belonged to the **kingdom Monera.**

Content Clues

Some scientists think there is a sixth kingdom made up of some organisms classfied now as **bacteria.**

A **phylum** is a smaller grouping of **organisms** within a kingdom. The kingdom Animalia has about 20 phyla. All animals that have backbones are part of the phylum called Chordata.

Practice

Genetic Information

The table below shows some dominant and recessive traits discovered in pea plants. Base your answers to questions 1–4 on this table and on your knowledge of science.

Traits in Pea Plants		
Trait	**Dominant**	**Recessive**
Seed shape	Round	Wrinkled
Seed color	Yellow	Green
Pod color	Green	Yellow
Flower color	Purple	White
Stem height	Tall	Short

1 What are two recessive traits of pea plants?

_____

 **Content Clue**

Recessive traits are not lost, just hidden. They may appear in later generations.

2 What can you infer from the table is a common type of reproduction in pea plants?

    1 asexual   3 cloning

    2 budding   4 sexual

3 If a pea plant that has two genes for round seeds is bred with a pea plant that has two genes for wrinkled seeds, what can you predict is the probability of each offspring having wrinkled seeds?

    1 75 percent   3 0 percent

    2 50 percent   4 100 percent

Content Clue

A **hybrid** is the **offspring** of two parents whose **genes** were pure but opposite for a trait.

4 Suppose every pea plant in your garden has a short stem. Short stem height is a recessive trait and should show up only in a small number of the plants. What other possible cause for this effect might there be besides inherited traits?

_____

_____

Practice

Change Over Time

Base your answers to questions 1–4 on the passage below.

The peregrine falcon is a beautiful bird of prey. It is blue gray with pointed wings and a black head and cheeks. This makes it look distinguished. Peregrine falcons are strong and fast. They fly high and dive at tremendous speeds. They live in open country and in cities.

By 1970, peregrine falcons were near extinction because of their exposure to a harmful pesticide called DDT. This would have been terrible. There were only 39 pairs of peregrine falcons left. The use of DDT was banned in the United States in 1972. After the ban, the number of peregrine falcons increased. By 1980, there were 99 pairs, and by 1998, there were 1,659 pairs. Their numbers will continue to increase.

> **Content Clue**
>
> DDT made the eggshells break easily. This usually resulted in the death of the developing bird.

1 What are the habitats of the peregrine falcon?

_____

2 What caused the near-extinction of the peregrine falcon?

_____

_____

_____

3 List two facts about peregrine falcons that appear in this passage.

_____

_____

_____

4 List two opinions about peregrine falcons that appear in this passage.

_____

_____

_____

> **Test Tip**
>
> When deciding between fact and opinion, look for words that describe, or adjectives.

Practice

Reproduction and Development

For questions 1 and 2, choose the best answer.

1 The changes a frog undergoes between the tadpole stage and the adult stage are known as

    1 maturation   3 metamorphosis

    2 revolution   4 classification

2 Frogs spend a lot of their lives on land. Their eggs, however, hatch in water, and their young develop in water. Frogs are

    1 mammals   3 reptiles

    2 marsupials   4 amphibians

Content Clues

Amphibians need to lay their eggs in water because the eggs do not have shells to protect them.

A complete **metamorphosis** usually includes a change in behavior or **environment** as well as a change in body shape.

Base your answers to questions 3–5 on the diagram below and on your knowledge of science. Write your answers in the space provided.

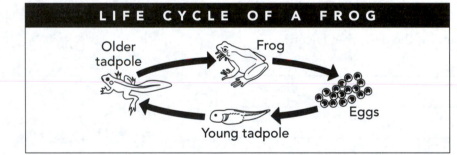

LIFE CYCLE OF A FROG

Older tadpole — Frog — Eggs — Young tadpole

3 Compare the body structures of tadpoles and adult frogs.

_____

_____

Content Clue

Often the shape of something is related to how it works.

4 Compare the way tadpoles and adult frogs breathe.

_____

_____

Test Tip

Use your powers of observation as you study the diagram to find ways tadpoles and adult frogs are alike and different.

5 Compare the way tadpoles and adult frogs move around.

_____

_____

Practice

Meeting Daily Needs

Below is a table that shows how minerals and vitamins are used by the human body. Base your answers to questions 1–3 on the data in the table and on your general knowledge of science.

Vitamins		Minerals	
Vitamin	Used for	Mineral	Used for

A	Normal sight
	Healthy skin
	Defense against
	    infection
		Potassium	Nerve and
			    muscle
			    functions

B	Nerve and heart
	    functions
		Calcium	Bone and
			    tooth growth

C	Tissue growth
	Healing wounds
		Iron	Forming red
			    blood and
			    muscle cells

D	Bone growth and repair		

1 Which vitamin is most important for maintaining healthy eyes?

    1 B   3 A
    2 C   4 D

2 Which nutrients are most important for bone growth?

    1 vitamin A and iron   3 vitamin B and potassium
    2 vitamin D and calcium   4 vitamin C and iron

3 Vitamins B and C dissolve in water. This means your body does not store them. Explain what you can infer from this about the foods you need to eat every day.

_____

_____

_____

> **Content Clue**
>
> Vitamins A and D are fat-soluble. This means your body can store them.

4 Lack of eating a particular nutrient can lead to what is called a deficiency disease. An example of a vitamin deficiency disease is

    1 diabetes   3 influenza
    2 rickets   4 allergies

Practice

Energy in Ecosystems

Base your answers to questions 1–4 on the passage below.

Many organisms get food by eating other organisms. An organism that eats other organisms is a consumer. Rabbits eat grass and other plants. Rabbits are primary consumers. A primary consumer is an organism that eats producers. A producer is an organism, such as a plant, that makes its own food.

Consumers that eat primary consumers are secondary consumers. Consumers that eat secondary consumers are tertiary consumers. Hawks eat small meat-eating animals, such as weasels. Hawks are tertiary consumers. Some animals, such as hawks, are also secondary consumers. Most humans are primary, secondary, and tertiary consumers.

Test Tip

If you are allowed to write in your test booklet, sometimes it helps to make notes in the margin as you read long passages.

Content Clue

Scavengers and **decomposers** eat or break down the remains and wastes of other **organisms.**

1 What can you infer about tertiary consumers?
1 They are also producers.
2 They are eaten by secondary consumers.
3 They are at the top of the energy pyramid.
4 They are rabbits.

2 Compare a producer with a consumer.

_____

3 How would you classify humans?
1 plant-eating animals
2 primary, secondary, and tertiary consumers
3 primary consumers
4 secondary consumers

4 Suppose the secondary and tertiary consumers were removed from this ecosystem. Which of the following predictions is most reasonable?
1 The number of primary consumers would increase.
2 The number of producers would increase.
3 The number of primary consumers would decrease.
4 The number of primary consumers would remain the same.

Practice

Humans and the Environment

For questions 1–4, choose the best answer. For question 5, write your answer on a separate sheet of paper.

1 The major cause of air pollution is
    1 the cutting down of trees
    2 the burning of fossil fuels
    3 global warming
    4 overpopulation

Content Clue

Cars and factories are the main sources of air **pollution** and **acid rain.**

2 Without carbon dioxide in the atmosphere, most of the Sun's energy would escape into space. Instead, carbon dioxide reflects the energy back to the Earth. What is this called?
    1 the ozone layer
    2 the greenhouse effect
    3 the carbon dioxide cycle
    4 refraction

3 Scientists have observed another problem caused by air pollution. The ozone layer of the atmosphere, which normally filters out harmful radiation from the Sun, is damaged by air pollution. Based on this information, which prediction best describes the problem?
    1 If air pollution increases, the ozone layer may get thicker.
    2 If air pollution decreases, the ozone layer may get thinner.
    3 If air pollution increases, more people may get skin cancer.
    4 If air pollution decreases, more people may get skin cancer.

Content Clue

Ozone is a type of **oxygen molecule** that forms when **ultraviolet radiation** strikes oxygen in the upper **atmosphere.** Some aerosol sprays and refrigerants (CFCs) contain chemicals that break down ozone.

4 A major cause of water pollution is
    1 fertilizers and pesticides washed off farm fields
    2 overuse of water in urban areas
    3 damming up rivers to form reservoirs
    4 introducing exotic species into the environment

5 Some greenhouse effect is necessary for life to exist on Earth. Too much greenhouse effect, however, can harm life on Earth by causing global warming. On a separate sheet of paper, explain the relationship between burning fossil fuels and global warming.

Content Clue

The study of the relationship between living things and their **environment** is called **ecology.**

Practice

The Earth and Space

Base your answers to questions 1–4 on the table below, which compares the Earth to the Moon.

	Earth	**Moon**
Age	4.5 billion years	4.5 billion years
Rotation period	24 hours	27.3 days
Surface area	510 million km²	38 million km²
Circumference	40,075 km	10,927 km

1 The Moon's period of revolution around the Earth is about 27.3 days. Which statement is best supported by the data in the table?

  1 The Moon's year is equal to its day.

  2 The Moon's rotation period is the same as its period of revolution around the Earth.

  3 The Moon takes as long to spin on its axis as it does to go around the Sun.

  4 The Earth and the Moon have about the same length of day.

2 Based on the data in the table, which of the following statements is the most reasonable inference?

  1 The Moon is much bigger than the Earth.

  2 Rotation period is another way of saying "day-night cycle."

  3 The Moon has half the surface area of the Earth.

  4 Surface area is another way of saying "circumference."

3 What can you infer about the Earth and the Moon based on the age data in the chart?

  1 The Earth and the Moon formed at about the same time.

  2 The Earth is much older than the Moon.

  3 The Moon is much older than the Earth.

  4 The Moon is made of the same material as the Earth is.

4 On a separate sheet of paper, use the data in the table to write a paragraph that compares the Earth to the Moon. In what ways are they alike? In what ways are they different?

 **Test Tip**

Read long questions and answers carefully. Try to eliminate some answer choices by picking out key words. The Sun isn't mentioned anywhere in the table, so you can probably eliminate choice 3.

Content Clue

One theory states that a giant **asteroid** hit the Earth in our distant past and broke off the piece that became the Moon.

Practice

The Interaction of Air, Land, and Water

Base your answers to questions 1–3 on the weather map below.

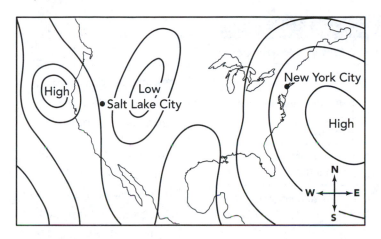

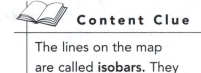

Content Clue

The lines on the map are called **isobars.** They connect areas of like pressure.

1 In the Northern Hemisphere, wind circulates in a counter-clockwise direction in a low pressure area and in a clockwise direction in a high pressure area. Which of the following inferences is the most reasonable?

    1 The wind in Salt Lake City is blowing from the north.
    2 The wind in Salt Lake City is blowing from the south.
    3 The wind in Salt Lake City is blowing from the east.
    4 The wind in Salt Lake City is blowing from the west.

2 A low pressure area usually means rainy or stormy weather, and a high pressure area usually means clear weather. Compare the weather in Salt Lake City with the weather in New York City.

_____

_____

_____

3 Predict what kind of weather Salt Lake City will be having soon. How do you know?

_____

_____

_____

_____

Content Clue

Weather systems usually move from west to east in North America.

Practice

Physical Properties of Matter

Base your answers to questions 1–4 on the table below, which shows five unknown mineral samples.

Classifying Minerals			
Mineral	**Color**	**Hardness**	**Other Properties**
Sample 1	Bright yellow	2.5	Shiny
Sample 2	Clear	10.0	8-sided crystals
Sample 3	Bright yellow	6.5	Shiny
Sample 4	Black	6.0	12-sided crystals, magnetic
Sample 5	Black	6.0	12-sided crystals

Content Clues

Minerals are classified by their **properties.** Two of those properties are hardness and color.

Mineral hardness is rated on a scale of 1 to 10. The softest rating is 1. Talc has a hardness of 1. The hardest rating is 10. Diamond has a hardness of 10.

1 Compare the mineral samples in the table. Which of the following statements is the most accurate comparison?

   1 Sample 5 is exactly the same as Sample 4.

   2 Sample 2 is the hardest mineral and Sample 1 is the softest.

   3 Sample 1 and Sample 3 are probably the same mineral.

   4 Sample 4 is harder than Sample 2.

2 Analyzing the data in the table and using your knowledge of science, what can you infer about the mineral samples?

   1 Sample 2 is probably a diamond.

   2 Sample 2 is the softest mineral and Sample 1 is the hardest.

   3 Sample 5 is probably gold.

   4 Sample 3 has more mass than Sample 5.

3 Arrange the mineral samples in order of hardness, beginning with the hardest.

_____

_____

_____

Test Tip

When being asked to arrange objects in order, be absolutely sure of the order you need to put the objects in. Although it might seem more natural, for question 3 don't start with the softest mineral and work your way up to the hardest.

4 If Sample 4 and Sample 5 were broken up and mixed together, how could you separate them?

_____

_____

Practice

Forms of Energy

Base your answers to questions 1–3 on the diagrams below, which show some different forms of energy.

Content Clues

Nuclear energy is **energy** stored in the **nucleus** of an **atom**.

Chemical energy is stored in **molecules**.

Light energy is energy in the form of moving waves of light.

Heat energy is energy in the form of moving molecules.

Potential energy is energy that is stored in **matter**.

1 Compare the diagrams. Which of the following statements is the most reasonable inference?

   1 The plant is converting light energy to chemical energy.

   2 The boy is converting chemical energy to nuclear energy.

   3 The candle is converting heat energy to light energy.

   4 The lawnmower is converting chemical energy to electrical energy.

2 Which two diagrams show energy being stored as chemical and potential energy?

   1 Figure 1 and Figure 3

   2 Figure 5 and Figure 6

   3 Figure 2 and Figure 4

   4 Figure 4 and Figure 6

3 Analyze the diagrams. Do you see a relationship between Figure 1 and Figure 3? If there is a relationship, what sort of energy transformation is taking place?

_____

_____

_____

Practice

Forces and Motion

Base your answers to questions 1–3 on the diagram below, which compares a man's weight on the Earth to his weight on the Moon.

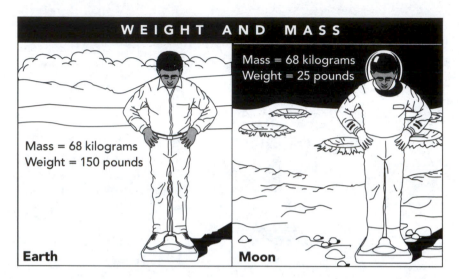

WEIGHT AND MASS

Mass = 68 kilograms
Weight = 25 pounds

Mass = 68 kilograms
Weight = 150 pounds

Earth

Moon

Content Clue

Weight changes relative to gravitational pull. **Mass** always remains constant.

1 Based on the diagram, which of the following statements is the most reasonable inference?

   1 The Moon has about the same mass as the Earth.

   2 The Moon has about half the mass of the Earth.

   3 The Moon has about one-sixth the mass of the Earth.

   4 The Moon has about one-eighth the mass of the Earth.

Content Clue

Mass is the amount of **matter** in an object. The more mass an object has, the greater the **force** of its **gravity**.

2 The measure of the force of gravity on an object is its weight. The stronger the pull, the greater the weight. Compare the mass and weight of the man on Earth and on the Moon. Explain why his mass is the same but his weight is different.

_____

_____

_____

_____

Test Tip

Always try to write answers in complete sentences. This helps to improve the quality of your thinking as well as of your writing.

3 If the man in the diagram were transported to a planet with half the mass of the Earth, what would his mass be? What would his weight be?

_____

CHAPTER 6

Interpreting and Analyzing Data

Much of what you study in science is presented as discussion or explanations in your textbook. However, scientific information can often be presented in other ways to make it easier to understand.

Picturing Facts

Tables, charts, and graphs help you picture a collection of facts on a topic. Tables are made up of columns and rows. Columns run vertically (up and down) and rows run horizontally (across or left to right). Both columns and rows divide data into categories. A calendar, for example, has columns that separate the days of the week and rows that separate the weeks of the month.

The first step in reading a table, chart, or graph is to identify its subject or topic. Often this information can be found in the title.

Example The chart below shows wind chill temperatures. The wind chill factor is the cooling effect the wind seems to have when temperatures are low.

The first column lists the actual air temperatures. The other columns show what happens when air is moving at certain speeds.

Look at the second column. It tells you that when the air is moving at 8 kilometers per hour, and the actual air temperature is $-7°C$, it feels as if it is $-9°C$. The last column tells you that when air is moving at 40 kilometers per hour, the air feels as if it is $-26°C$. What does the third column show? _____

Wind Chill Temperatures					
Actual Temperature (°C)	**Wind Speed (kilometers per hour)**				
	8	**16**	**24**	**32**	**40**
−7	−9	−15	−20	−18	−26
−12	−14	−22	−27	−31	−33
−17	−20	−29	−37	−39	−42
−23	−26	−36	−42	−47	−50

Tables and Charts

Tables and charts make it fast and easy to compare information. A table or chart usually presents information by grouping it into rows and columns. At the top of each column is a column heading. The heading tells you what is in that column. On the left side of the table may be row headings. A row heading tells you what is in the row.

Tables usually show numerical data, such as height, depth, length, and weight. Information can be arranged in a table in chronological, or time, order to show patterns or trends. For example, a table showing the size of certain animal populations over a period of years can indicate patterns of rising or falling numbers.

Data Tables A chart will use more words or pictures than a table, but some tables do use words rather than numerical data. A text table, for example, might show the decline in several different species by listing them in certain categories.

Example Look at the table below, which lists U.S. animal species in trouble or already extinct. What are the headings for the columns?

_____

What do these headings tell you about what is in these columns?

_____

_____

In what category is the Florida manatee? _____

Extinct, Endangered, and Threatened Animals of the United States		
Extinct	**Endangered**	**Threatened**
Caribbean monk seal	Jaguarundi	American alligator
Mexican grizzly bear	Ridley's sea turtle	Bald eagle
Passenger pigeon	Florida manatee	California sea otter
Steller's sea cow	Mexican wolf	Peregrine falcon

Punnett Squares Punnett squares are charts that use letters to represent the genes that offspring will inherit. Punnett squares indicate whether gene pairs are dominant, recessive, or a hybrid. They are used to figure out the probability of a trait being passed on.

Content Clue

Over many generations a **species** can adapt to a changing **environment**. However, **pollution** and other types of damage caused by human activity change the environment too quickly for many plant or animal populations to adapt.

Content Clue

Species are threatened if their numbers are decreasing and they could eventually become **extinct**. Species are **endangered** if they are in immediate danger of becoming extinct. Even with human help, these species may not survive.

Graphs

Graphs can show the same information found in a table. However, graphs usually present data in a more interesting way. Bar graphs, line graphs, and pie graphs often use special color, shading, or patterns to show information. Keys indicate what the colors, shades, or patterns represent.

Bar Graphs Bar graphs show a relationship between groups. Bar graphs are a fast way to show big differences. A bar graph displays information as a series of bars, or columns.

Example Look at the bar graph shown below. What do the numbers on the left side represent? _____

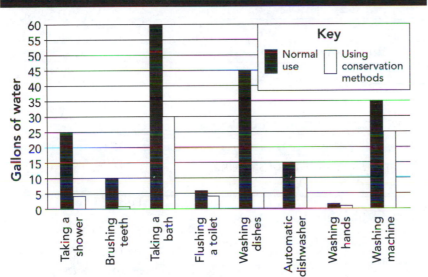

Test Tip

To read a bar graph, you must find the point at which the information plotted on both axes meets.

Line Graphs Like bar graphs, line graphs provide a fast and easy way to represent data. In many cases data plotted on a bar graph also can be plotted on a line graph.

Line graphs are made using a grid formed by the horizontal (x) axis and the vertical (y) axis. Often, the x-axis indicates time. The y-axis indicates a quantity.

To read a line graph, you must find the point at which the information plotted on both axes meets. Lines connecting the plotted points help highlight trends and patterns. A sharply sloping line, for example, shows a rapid rate of change.

Example Look at the line graph below. What type of information does the *x*-axis show? _____

Does Tracy's heart rate show rapid change? _____

If so, at what point? _____

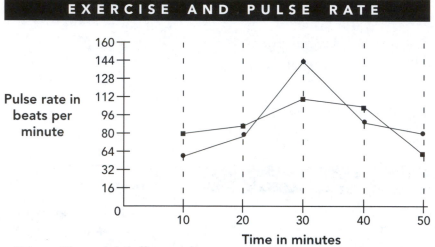

EXERCISE AND PULSE RATE

Pulse rate in beats per minute

Time in minutes

- Tracy - 36-year-old office worker
- Albert - 26-year-old former college athlete

Pie Graphs A pie graph shows how a part of something relates to the whole. Pie graphs are often referred to as pie *charts,* but they are really graphs. This type of graph is a good way of showing percentages.

Example Look at the pie graph below. Which fuel is used most widely in the United States? _____

Nuclear power makes up what percentage of energy use? _____

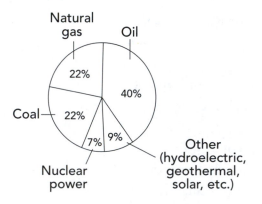

FUEL USE IN THE UNITED STATES

Natural gas

Oil

22%

40%

Coal 22%

7% 9%

Nuclear power

Other (hydroelectric, geothermal, solar, etc.)

✏️ **Test Tip**

Pie graphs use either keys below or "pie cut" lines inside the pie to show how much each piece of the pie represents.

📖 **Content Clue**

Nuclear fission is the process used to produce **nuclear energy** for fuel. The process splits the **nucleus** of **atoms**, which releases **energy**.

Practice

Living and Nonliving Things

Susan had two slides of unknown cells. She created this chart about her observations of each one.

Base your answers to questions 1–4 on this chart.

The Cell			
Cell Part Found	**Cell A**	**Cell B**	**Function**
Cell membrane	✔	✔	Controls what goes into and out of the cell
Nucleus	✔	✔	Controls cell activities
Cytoplasm	✔	✔	Contains organelles
Mitochondrion	✔	✔	Provides energy
Vacuole	✔	✔	Stores food, water, and minerals
Chloroplast		✔	Makes food during photosynthesis
Cell wall		✔	Gives shape and support
Ribosome	✔	✔	Produces proteins

Content Clue

Chloroplasts contain the green pigment chlorophyll. Chlorophyll is used in photosynthesis.

1 Which cell part is present in Cell B but not in Cell A?

   1 chloroplast   3 mitochondrion

   2 ribosome   4 vacuole

2 Based on your answer to question 1, what does the absence of this cell part tell you about Cell A?

3 How do mitochondria and ribosomes differ in terms of function?

4 Based on the information in the table, what conclusion could you draw about Cells A and B?

Test Tip

A chart will not always give you all the information you need. Sometimes you must make **inferences** or predictions. Or, you may need to draw conclusions based on data in the table and on what you know already.

Practice

Genetic Information

Punnett squares are charts that show the probability of inheriting a trait. Marco and Sandy are married and planning a family. What traits will their children have?

Base your answers to questions 1–5 on the Punnett squares and the information below.

Dominant genes
C = curly hair
D = dark hair
B = brown eyes

Recessive genes
c = straight hair
d = blonde hair
b = blue eyes

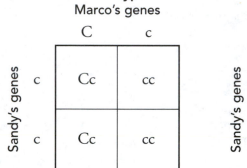
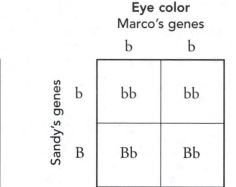

1 What are Marco's genes for hair type?

_____

2 What color hair does Sandy have?

_____

3 What is the probability that Marco's and Sandy's offspring will have straight hair?

_____

4 What is the probability that their offspring will have dark hair?

_____

5 What is the probability that their offspring will have brown eyes?

_____

Practice

Change Over Time

The data below were obtained when a neighborhood was sprayed with insecticide to control mosquitoes. Spraying took place on Day 1 only. The population numbers were obtained by capturing mosquitoes in a trap placed in the center of the neighborhood.

Base your answers to questions 1 and 2 on the data and on the resulting graph. The number under each day represents the number of mosquitoes.

Day 1	Day 5	Day 10	Day 15	Day 20
1,000	500	5	100	300

1 In the grid provided, make a line graph of the data showing the change in the mosquito population over the 20 days studied.

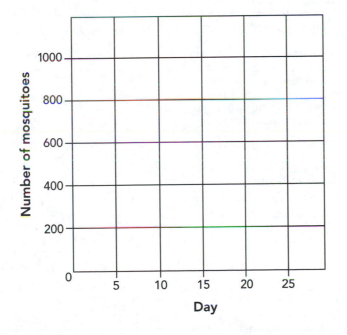

Test Tips

Start by plotting the population using points. Then connect the points with a ruler.

Sometimes a grid will not provide space for every number you need to plot. In those cases, you have to estimate.

2 Read each statement. Which one is a reasonable inference that can be made from the line graph?
  1 The mosquito population begins to increase after Day 10.
  2 Spraying with insecticide has no effect on mosquito population numbers.
  3 Mosquitoes develop a resistance to insecticide after 10 days.
  4 The mosquito population continued to decline after Day 10.

Practice

Reproduction and Development

A chicken embryo takes about 20 days to develop into a chick in the egg. The mother keeps the egg warm during this development by incubating it. That means she keeps it warm with her body heat.

Base your answers to questions 1–4 on the chart below.

Chicken Embryo Development		
Day	Embryo A	Embryo B
1	First signs of head, backbone, blood vessels, eyes	First signs of head and backbone; no blood vessels or eyes present
5	Heart present and beating; first signs of nose, legs, and wings; reproductive organs present	Heart present and beating but irregular; blood vessels present; no sign of reproductive organs
10	Beak has hardened and egg tooth has formed; feathers have formed	Nose, legs, and wings have begun to form; first signs of beak and feathers
15	Scales and claws are present	Heartbeat still irregular; legs not properly developed; scales and claws are present
20	Embryo almost size of shell; yolk sac has been absorbed; ready to hatch	Embryo half the size of the shell; no sign of hatching

 **Content Clues**

While it is developing into a chick, the embryo feeds on the yolk sac inside the egg.

The baby chick breaks out of the shell using a structure called the *egg tooth*. This tooth falls off soon after the chick hatches.

1 At what point does Embryo A have a beating heart?

_____

2 How big is Embryo B on Day 20?

_____

Test Tip

Question 3 is really asking you to *analyze* the data in the chart.

3 Based on the data in the chart, which embryo do you think is developing normally?

_____

Content Clue

During incubation, eggs are kept at a temperature of exactly 27°C. Cooler or warmer temperatures result in slow growth and possible death of the embryo.

4 Explain what you think might have caused the differences in the developing embryos. _____

_____

_____

Practice

Meeting Daily Needs

Base your answers to questions 1–3 on the chart below.

Vitamin	What It Does	Source	Problems Caused by Deficiency
A (retinol)	Keeps skin and eyes healthy and helps growth of bones	Yellow and dark green vegetables, yellow fruit	Night blindness, dry eyes, eye infections, dry skin
B$_1$	Helps body get energy from food	Whole grains, meat, potatoes, eggs	Tiredness, lack of sleep, leg cramps and weakness; beriberi
B$_{12}$	Helps growth and formation of red blood cells	Eggs, milk, meat	Anemia
C (ascorbic acid)	Keeps gums healthy and helps wounds heal	Citrus fruits, tomatoes, green peppers, cabbage, broccoli	Scurvy (burst capillaries just under the surface of the skin; swollen, bleeding gums)
D	Helps body use calcium and phosphorus to keep bones and teeth healthy and strong	Egg yolks, butter, liver, fortified milk	Softening of bones called rickets in children

> **Content Clue**
>
> **Nutrients** include water, **carbohydrates, fats, proteins, minerals,** and **vitamins.**

1 What evidence would indicate a deficiency of vitamin A in a person's diet?

    1 problem with skin and eyes

    2 muscle weakness

    3 swollen gums

    4 leg cramps

2 Based on the information in the table, which of the following is a true statement?

    1 If you eat dark green vegetables, you will not suffer from a vitamin D deficiency.

    2 Milk is a good source of vitamin A.

    3 Eating eggs can prevent scurvy.

    4 A diet that does not include meat could lead to tiredness and anemia.

> **Content Clue**
>
> Vitamin D is also formed in the human skin as a result of exposure to sunlight.

3 On a separate sheet of paper, write what you can infer from this table about the importance of vitamins in your diet.

Practice

Energy in Ecosystems

Base your answers to questions 1–3 on the passage and the chart below.

A biologist studying wetland areas kept notes of what she observed in the shallow water of a tidal marsh. She noted that below the shallow water the soil was thin and poor. Most of the plants she saw were marsh grasses, which were being eaten by minnows. The minnows, in turn, were eaten by killifish and silverside fish. She marked off a 2-meter square and counted the life forms inside the square. She then made a table from her observations.

Test Tip

As you read the passage, sketch a **food web** or a **food chain** to see the relationships between the **organisms** in this **ecosystem**.

Content Clue

An ecosystem is all the living and nonliving things in an **environment**.

A Tidal Marsh Ecosystem		
Organism Observed	Number Counted or Estimated	Producer, Consumer, Decomposer, or Scavenger?
Algae (seaweed plants)	18	Producer
Marsh grass plants	83	Producer
Flat worm	50 (est)	Decomposer
Annelid (worms)	20	Decomposer/Consumer
Minnow	49	Consumer
Killifish	3	Consumer
Shrimp	8	Scavenger/Consumer
Silverside fish	1	Consumer

1 In numbers of individuals, which type of organism is the most common in this ecosystem?

    1 consumer   3 producer

    2 scavenger   4 decomposer

2 On a separate sheet of paper, use the data in the table and the passage above it to describe a food chain in this ecosystem.

3 Minnows, silverside fish, and killifish are all consumers. On the same sheet of paper, explain why there are so many more minnows than silverside fish and killifish in this ecosystem.

Practice

Humans and the Environment

Base your answers to questions 1–4 on the line graph below.

Examine the figures showing the average annual temperature in the United States. Then answer the questions that follow.

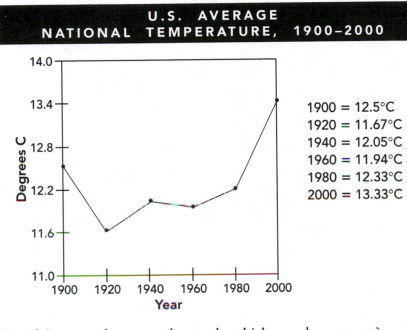

U.S. AVERAGE NATIONAL TEMPERATURE, 1900–2000

1900 = 12.5°C
1920 = 11.67°C
1940 = 12.05°C
1960 = 11.94°C
1980 = 12.33°C
2000 = 13.33°C

Test Tip

To understand what a line graph is showing, look at the plotted points along the vertical and horizontal axes.

1 Of the years shown on the graph, which was the warmest?

  1 1900   3 1980

  2 1940   4 2000

2 Between which years did the average annual temperature increase the most?

  1 1900 to 1920   3 1920 to 1940

  2 1960 to 1980   4 1980 to 2000

3 Based on the information in the graph and your knowledge of current society, what do you expect will happen to the temperature by the year 2020?

_____

4 What do you conclude may have caused the increase in the temperature shown in the graph? Explain your answer.

_____

Content Clues

An increase in greenhouse gases in the **atmosphere** could cause an overall rise in the **temperature** of the planet.

The greenhouse gases include **carbon dioxide**, water vapor, and methane.

Practice

The Earth and Space

Base your answers to questions 1–5 on the chart below.

The Planets			
Planets	**Distance from Sun**	**Length of Day**	**Length of Year**
Mercury	58 million km	59 Earth days	88 Earth days
Venus	108 million km	243 Earth days	225 Earth days
Earth	150 million km	24 Earth hours	365 Earth days
Mars	228 million km	25 Earth hours	687 Earth days
Jupiter	778 million km	10 Earth hours	12 Earth years
Saturn	1.4 billion km	10 Earth hours	29 Earth years
Uranus	2.9 billion km	17 Earth hours	84 Earth years
Neptune	4.5 billion km	19 Earth hours	165 Earth years
Pluto	5.9 billion km	6 Earth days	248 Earth years

> **Content Clue**
>
> The lengths of days or years for all the planets is given in terms of Earth hours, days, and years. This makes it easier for the reader to form a mental picture.

> **Test Tip**
>
> When studying the chart, look closely to distinguish *hours*, *days*, and *years*.

1 Which planet has been observed to have the shortest year?

  1 Mercury   3 Earth

  2 Jupiter   4 Venus

2 Which planet's day has been observed to be closest in length to an Earth day?

  1 Mercury   3 Mars

  2 Venus   4 Jupiter

3 The orbits of which planets are located farthest away from each other?

  1 Mercury and Venus   3 Mars and Jupiter

  2 Earth and Mars   4 Neptune and Pluto

4 Explain how the length of Venus' day and year differ from those of the other planets.

_____

> **Content Clue**
>
> The farther a planet is from the Sun, the longer its period of **revolution**, or year.

5 Explain why Pluto's period of revolution is the longest.

_____

Practice

The Interaction of Air, Land, and Water

Base your answers to questions 1–4 on the table below.

Top 10 U.S. Earthquakes		
Location	**Date**	**Magnitude**
Prince William Sound, Alaska	March 27, 1964	9.2
Andreanof Islands, Alaska	March 9, 1957	8.8
Rat Islands, Alaska	Feb. 4, 1965	8.7
Shumagin Islands, Alaska	Nov. 10, 1938	8.3
Lituya Bay, Alaska	July 10, 1958	8.3
Yakutat Bay, Alaska	Sept. 10, 1899	8.2
Cape Yakataga, Alaska	Sept. 4, 1899	8.2
Andreanof Islands, Alaska	May 7, 1986	8.0
New Madrid, Missouri	Feb. 7, 1812	7.9
Fort Tejon, California	Jan. 9, 1857	7.9

Content Clue

The **Richter scale** shows an **earthquake's** relative strength, or *magnitude.* For each one integer increase in number, the earthquake is said to be 10 times stronger. An earthquake with a Richter scale reading of 7 is 10 times stronger than an earthquake with a reading of 6.

1 According to the table, which state had the most recent earthquake? _____

2 How many times more powerful was the earthquake in Prince William Sound than the one in Yakutat Bay? _____

3 Which statement is best supported by data in the table?
  1 Alaska has more serious earthquakes than any other state.
  2 Alaska has fewer serious earthquakes than any other state.
  3 Alaska has as many serious earthquakes as most other states.
  4 California has more serious earthquakes than most other states.

4 Explain what you can infer about why there are so many earthquakes in Alaska.

_____

_____

_____

Content Clue

Most earthquakes occur where two sections of the Earth's **crust** meet. These are called tectonic **plates.** The coast of Alaska lies on the boundary between the North American and Pacific plates.

Practice

Physical Properties of Matter

Every substance requires a certain amount of heat to raise its temperature 1°C. The heat needed to raise 1 gram of a substance 1°C is called specific heat. Specific heat is a physical property. It can be used to identify a substance. Every substance has its own particular specific heat.

Base your answers to questions 1–3 on the bar graph below, which compares specific heats of several substances.

Content Clue

A **calorie** is the amount of **heat** needed to raise the **temperature** of 1 gram of water 1°C.

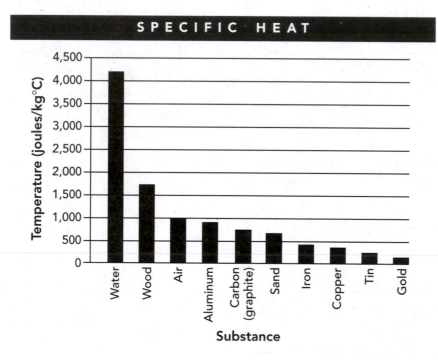

Test Tip

A bar graph is used to compare quantities. The longer the bar, the bigger the quantity.

1 Which substance shown in the bar graph has the highest specific heat? Which has the lowest?

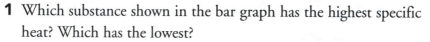

2 Specific heat can also be considered a measure of how quickly a substance transfers heat. A substance with a high specific heat transfers heat more slowly. Copper, for example, transfers heat more quickly than wood. Which substance transfers heat more slowly than wood?

3 On a separate sheet of paper, explain why the handles of metal cooking pots are sometimes made of wood.

Practice

Forms of Energy

Base your answers to questions 1–4 on the table below, which shows the rate at which sound travels through different materials.

The Speed of Sound	
Material	**Speed (meters/second)**
Dry air at 20°C	343
Plastic	540
Fresh water	1,497
Seawater	1,531
Gold	3,240
Wood	4,110
Glass	4,540
Steel	5,200

Content Clue

Most of the sound waves you hear travel through the air, but air isn't a very good **conductor** of sound. Sounds are much clearer when they travel through water, wood, or metal.

1 Sound travels fastest through
  1 dry air
  2 plastic
  3 glass
  4 steel

2 Sound travels slowest through
  1 water
  2 a window
  3 a frisbee
  4 a steel girder

Test Tip

The answer to a question isn't always found in the table. But you should be able to figure out the answer from the information in the table. This is part of analyzing or interpreting the **data**.

3 At what rate per hour does sound travel through dry air at 20°C?
  1 about 1,235 kilometers per hour
  2 about 74,088 kilometers per hour
  3 about 20.58 kilometers per hour
  4 about 20,580 kilometers per hour

4 Does sound travel faster through desert air or mountain air? Why?

_____

_____

Content Clue

Sound travels faster through warm air than through cold air. For example, the speed of sound increases from 343 meters per second at 20°C to 355 meters per second at 40°C.

Practice

Forces and Motion

Base your answers to questions 1–3 on the graph and on the table below.

A falling object accelerates as it falls. It does not fall at a constant velocity. The graph below shows the rate of change of velocity for a ball dropped from a tall building.

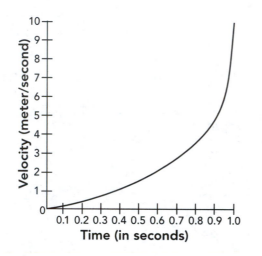

Content Clues

Speed is the measure of the distance an object moves in a given unit of time.

Velocity is speed in a definite direction.

Acceleration is a change in velocity over time. It may involve a change in speed or direction or both.

1 What is the force acting on the ball that changes its velocity as it falls? _____

2 As the ball accelerates, more distance is covered in each 0.1 second that passes. After 1 second, the ball has fallen 9.8 meters. What is its velocity at that point?

  1 9.8 meters/second   3 98 meters/second

  2 9.8 meters   4 0 meters/second

The ball's velocity was measured as it continued to fall. The data obtained was put into the following table:

Time (seconds)	Velocity (meters/second)
1	9.8
2	19.6
3	29.4

Test Tip

The graph stops at 1 second. The table begins at 1 second.

3 Acceleration describes how fast the velocity of a moving object is changing. How many meters per second does the ball's velocity change in 1 second? _____

CHAPTER 7

Designing Experiments

In experiments, you collect information under certain controlled conditions. The purpose of an experiment is to answer a question or test a possible answer to a question. After you do an experiment, you analyze your results. For example, you might be asked to design an experiment to find the best flour to use for chocolate chip cookies. Or, you might be asked to design an experiment to test whether a ping pong ball bounces higher than a golf ball. In both of these cases, you need to follow these basic steps:

- state a hypothesis
- identify variables
- develop a procedure
- gather data
- analyze results
- draw conclusions

This chapter will deal with the first three steps. These are the steps involved in designing an experiment.

State a Hypothesis

A hypothesis is a possible solution to the problem you want to solve or a possible answer to a question about the problem. Write out your hypothesis. This will keep you focused on the problem and help you decide what to test. A set of hypotheses that have held up under testing by many scientists is called a *theory*.

Example If you are testing chocolate chip cookies, you might write down this hypothesis:

> Chocolate chip cookies made with whole wheat flour are better than chocolate chip cookies made with white flour.

However, what do you mean by the word *better*? Do the cookies taste better? Are they cheaper or easier to make? Are they less likely to burn in the oven? Are they more nutritious? You need to make your hypothesis specific. A more testable hypothesis would be:

> Chocolate chip cookies made with whole wheat flour taste better than chocolate chip cookies made with white flour.

Test Tip

The Grade 8 Intermediate-Level Science Test may ask you to design an **experiment.** If you follow a certain procedure for doing experiments all the time, the question will not seem so difficult, no matter what the subject of the experiment is.

Content Clue

These steps are part of the process many scientists refer to as the **scientific method.**

Content Clue

In an experiment, test only one thing, or **variable,** at a time.

Example In the case of the ping pong ball and the golf ball, stating the hypothesis might seem very simple:

A ping pong ball bounces higher than a golf ball does.

However, do you mean that *this* ping pong ball bounces higher than *that* golf ball? Do you mean that *all* ping pong balls bounce higher than *all* golf balls? Or do you mean that, in general, ping pong balls bounce higher than golf balls?

The experiment you do will be a bit different for each case. If you want to know whether a certain ping pong ball bounces higher than a certain golf ball, you need to test only those two balls. If you want to know whether all ping pong balls bounce higher than all golf balls, you need to test a huge sample, including different brands of balls. If you want to know whether, in general, ping pong balls bounce higher than golf balls, you still need to test a large number of balls but not as many as for the second experiment.

Identify Variables

A variable is anything that can affect the outcome of the experiment. One of the variables in an experiment is the particular factor you are testing. This is the factor you will change during the experiment. Every variable that is *not* being tested needs to remain the same. A constant is a factor that does not change. If you don't have these constants, you will not be sure why you get the results you do.

Example In the cookie example, the factor being tested is the type of flour used. Suppose one batch of chocolate chip cookies uses white flour and butter. Another batch uses whole wheat flour and margarine. You think the first batch tastes better. Is the difference caused by the different flour or by the different fat? You have no way of knowing.

Suppose you make both batches using butter. However, in one batch you use 2 cups of whole wheat flour. In the other batch, you use $1\frac{1}{2}$ cups of white flour. This time the second batch tastes better. Is it because of the different *types* of flour or the different *amounts* of flour?

Content Clue

Science **experiments** are usually controlled. This means two setups are used. One setup, the control, is left alone. The experiment is done on the other setup. The experimental group can then be compared with the control group.

You must also make sure all the other ingredients are the same. For both batches, you need to use the same brand and type of sugar, the same grade of eggs, and the same brand of chocolate chips. In addition, you need to use the same amount of each ingredient for each of the different batches. The different batches need to be baked under the same conditions, at the same oven temperature, and for the same length of time. Everything about baking the two batches of cookies needs to be the same except the kind of flour used.

Example In the case of the bouncing balls, the factor to be varied is the type of ball—ping pong balls versus golf balls.

What are the variables that need to stay the same? Certainly the surface the balls are bounced on needs to be the same, as does the height from which the balls are dropped. Other factors may not be so obvious. Will the room temperature affect the way the balls bounce? What about humidity? What about time of day?

When you design an experiment, you need to take all the possible variables into account. If you decide not to ensure that a particular variable will remain constant, you need to have some idea of what effect this will have on the outcome of the experiment.

As much as possible, you want to control even the variables you think will have no effect on the outcome of the experiment. You may think that room temperature has no effect on the way balls bounce. However, most materials are affected by temperature. Extreme temperatures might change the results of this experiment. In this case, it is fairly easy to make sure the room temperature remains constant.

Identifying the variables that are not being tested and keeping them constant is one of the hardest parts of designing an experiment. When you design your experiment, write down all the possible variables. Then you will more easily see which factors you have to hold constant and which ones you will vary.

Develop a Procedure

Before you can do your experiment, you need to come up with a procedure. The best way to do this is to write down what you intend to do. What steps will you take that will allow you to vary the factor you are testing while keeping all the others constant?

Content Clue

Cooking food causes a **chemical change.** It turns the substance into something new. If you vary the ingredients, the chemical change may be different.

Test Tip

If you are not sure about whether a condition will affect the results of an **experiment,** try to keep it constant.

Test Tip

Use scrap paper to write down your thoughts on a procedure. Brainstorm all the possible steps. Then organize and eliminate.

The procedure must also provide a way to get meaningful results. For example, you may need to have measurements so you can compare things. In other cases, an experiment is testing to see only whether something happens or does not happen. In this case, measurements are not needed.

Example The procedure for testing the cookies needs to describe how you are going to make the two sets of cookies, keeping the variables other than flour type constant.

The procedure also needs to describe how you are going to measure your results. Once you have made your cookies, how are you going to decide which ones taste better? You could taste them yourself. However, that would be only one opinion. To get a scientifically meaningful result, you would need to ask many people to taste the cookies. In this case, you could ask ten of your friends to try both kinds of cookies and record which one they preferred.

Example The procedure for testing ping pong balls versus golf balls needs to define the surface on which the balls are being dropped and the height from which they are being dropped. The procedure should state the number of balls to be tested. The more balls you test, the better your results will be. However, ten ping pong balls and ten golf balls should probably give you meaningful results.

The procedure also needs to specify how you are going to measure the height each ball bounces. One possibility would be to place a meter stick behind each ball and have someone record the height on the meter stick to which each ball bounces.

Test Tip

Part of designing an **experiment** is figuring out how the results will answer the original question. In other words, how will you draw conclusions from your experiment?

Write It Down

As you practice designing experiments, get used to writing down every step of your plan. Write down your hypothesis. Write down the variables in your experiment. Write down a step-by-step procedure for performing your experiment.

Writing down everything makes it easier to actually do the experiment and keep track of what you have done. It helps you analyze your data. It also allows someone else to repeat your experiment and check your results. Finally, it will make it easier for you to successfully complete this part of the Grade 8 Intermediate-Level Science Test.

Test Tip

It is always a good idea to repeat an experiment many times to confirm your results.

Practice

Living and Nonliving Things

Kevin knows that he breathes faster after he runs. He guesses that the length of time he runs has an effect on how fast he breathes.

Design an experiment to see whether Kevin's guess was correct. Write your answers in the spaces provided. Include these elements in your response:

Hypothesis: _____

_____

_____

_____

Factor to be varied: _____

_____

Two factors to be held constant:

1 _____

2 _____

Procedure: _____

_____

_____

_____

_____

_____

_____

📖 **Content Clue**

Regular exercise strengthens the heart and lungs. A stronger heart pumps more blood with each beat. This lets the heart beat less often, which means the body doesn't need to breathe as fast.

✏️ **Test Tip**

If your **experiment** seems to need it, be sure to include a way to measure something. Here, you would need to measure how fast Kevin breathes. Also, remember to include the unit of measurement, such as breaths per minute.

Practice

Genetic Information

Devon notices that his garden has more red carnations than white carnations. He guesses that red is a dominant trait in carnations and white is recessive.

Design an experiment to see whether Devon's guess was correct. Write your answers in the spaces provided. Include these elements in your response:

Hypothesis: _____

_____

_____

_____

Factor to be varied: _____

_____

Two factors to be held constant:

1 _____

2 _____

Procedure: _____

_____

_____

_____

_____

_____

_____

_____

_____

Content Clue

If red is a **dominant trait** in carnations and white is a **recessive trait,** the chances are greater that the **offspring** of crossed red and white carnations will have red flowers rather than white flowers.

Test Tip

Write down a step-by-step plan for the procedure. Number your steps, and make sure they follow a logical order. Picture someone else trying to follow your directions. This will help you be clear and provide all the needed information.

Practice

Change Over Time

Marcia planted two different varieties of tomatoes in her garden. She planted all the Zing tomatoes together in one patch. All the Berry Red tomatoes were planted together in another patch. The Zing tomatoes grew taller and produced more tomatoes than the Berry Red plants. She guessed that this was because the Zing tomatoes were better adapted to growing in her area, which had a warmer climate, and that the Berry Red tomatoes were better adapted to growing in a colder climate.

Design an experiment to see whether Marcia's guess was correct. Write your answers in the spaces provided. Include these elements in your response:

Hypothesis: _____

_____

_____

_____

Factor to be varied: _____

_____

Two factors to be held constant:

1 _____

2 _____

Procedure: _____

_____

_____

_____

_____

_____

_____

_____

Content Clue

Marcia is going to need to find someone in a colder **climate** to help her test her **hypothesis.** She is going to have to supply her helper with lots of information to make sure all the necessary **variables** are controlled.

Test Tip

You do not need to prove a hypothesis right or wrong. You need only to see whether your findings support or fail to support your hypothesis.

Practice

Reproduction and Development

One day Jeremy was observing the caterpillars in his yard. He saw that fifteen of them had formed cocoons. He guessed that the cocoons would develop faster if they were kept warmer.

Design an experiment to see whether Jeremy's guess was correct. Write your answers in the spaces provided. Include these elements in your response:

Hypothesis: _____

_____

_____

_____

Factor to be varied: _____

_____

Two factors to be held constant:

1 _____

2 _____

Procedure: _____

_____

_____

_____

_____

_____

_____

_____

_____

Test Tip

It can be difficult to think of all possible factors. Think of the **environment** as one group of factors. When doing **experiments** with living things, an **organism's** internal conditions are also factors.

Content Clue

Jeremy will need to collect caterpillars so he can find out the time at which each one develops and makes its cocoon. He will also need to be able to tell the cocoons apart, so he will need to mark them somehow.

Practice

Meeting Daily Needs

Sarah grew lilies in her garden. She had read about three different kinds of fertilizers. She had an idea about which would be best to use on her flowers. She thought that "Type 1" would be the best fertilizer.

Design an experiment to see whether Sarah's guess was correct. Write your answers in the spaces provided. Include these elements in your response:

Hypothesis: _____

_____

_____

_____

Factor to be varied: _____

_____

Two factors to be held constant:

1 _____

2 _____

Procedure: _____

_____

_____

_____

_____

_____

_____

_____

_____

> **Content Clue**
>
> Fertilizers are natural or artificial substances added to **soil.** They contain chemicals to improve plant growth.

> **Test Tip**
>
> There may be many **variables** that need to be held constant. If the question only asks for two, pick the two you think are the most important.

> **Test Tip**
>
> Make sure the plants to be tested are about the same size when you start.

Practice

Energy in Ecosystems

Patrick got a terrarium as a birthday present from his friend Josh, who already had one. Patrick noticed that his terrarium did not last as long as Josh's. The plants inside it died. He wondered if this was because his terrarium did not have any animals.

Design an experiment to see whether Patrick's guess was correct. Write your answers in the spaces provided. Include these elements in your response:

Hypothesis: _____

_____

_____

_____

Factor to be varied: _____

_____

Two factors to be held constant:

1 _____

2 _____

Procedure: _____

_____

_____

_____

_____

_____

_____

_____

📖 **Content Clue**

In an **ecosystem**, **producers** and **consumers** depend on each other. Producers give off **oxygen** that consumers breathe in. Consumers give off **carbon dioxide** that plants use for **photosynthesis**.

✏️ **Test Tips**

Your procedure will need to include a way to record **data**.

Also, be sure to note what each plant looks like at the beginning of the **experiment** so its growth can be compared with the growth of the other plants.

Practice

Humans and the Environment

Jason noticed that the pond near his house had developed a thick covering of algae. The growth seemed to have developed only after the golf course had been built. He thought that the fertilizer used on the grass at the golf course might have caused the algae growth in the pond.

Design an experiment to see whether Jason's guess was correct. Write your answers in the spaces provided. Include these elements in your response:

Hypothesis: _____

_____

_____

_____

Factor to be varied: _____

_____

Two factors to be held constant:

1 _____

2 _____

Procedure: _____

_____

_____

_____

_____

_____

_____

_____

_____

> **Content Clue**
>
> Fertilizer used on grass usually contains nitrogen and phosphorus, two things **algae** need to live and grow.

> **Test Tip**
>
> Don't forget that observation is an important part of most scientific procedures.

Practice

The Earth and Space

One day Tony noticed that in his town, the shortest shadows of the day occurred at 11:30 A.M. rather than at 12:00 noon. This told him that in his town, noon in solar time was different from noon on his clock. He guessed that the difference between what the clock showed as noon and what the Sun showed as noon was the same all year round.

Design an experiment to see whether Tony's guess was correct. Write your answers in the spaces provided. Include these elements in your response:

Hypothesis: _____

_____

_____

_____

Factor to be varied: _____

_____

Two factors to be held constant:

1 _____

2 _____

Procedure: _____

_____

_____

_____

_____

_____

_____

_____

_____

📖 Content Clue

In ancient times, people used the Sun and the shadows that it created to tell time. This is called *solar time*. Because of the Earth's **rotation,** the Sun changes position in the sky as the day goes on. Normally, the shortest shadows occur at 12:00 noon, solar time.

✏️ Test Tip

You do not need to always follow the steps of the **scientific method** exactly in designing your **experiment.** You may skip some or repeat some others. It all depends on the problem you are trying to solve. However, don't eliminate any step without giving it careful thought.

✏️ Test Tip

Although checking the shadows every day would be ideal for this experiment, doing it once a week is probably often enough.

Practice

The Interaction of Air, Land, and Water

Selena noticed that the sand at the beach seemed much warmer than the water. She wondered whether that was because water took more energy to heat up than land.

Design an experiment to see whether Selena's guess was correct. Write your answers in the spaces provided. Include these elements in your response:

Hypothesis: _____

_____

_____

_____

Factor to be varied: _____

_____

Two factors to be held constant:

1 _____

2 _____

Procedure: _____

_____

_____

_____

_____

_____

_____

_____

_____

_____

Content Clue

Sunlight is a form of **radiation.** Radiation is the transfer of **energy** in the form of **waves.** Different substances absorb radiation at different rates.

Test Tip

Be sure to always put your **hypothesis** in a form that can be tested by your **experiment.**

Practice

Physical Properties of Matter

Frances took swimming lessons in a swimming pool. Then her family went to the beach, and she swam in the ocean. She noticed that her body seemed lighter in the ocean than it had seemed in the pool, which made it easier for her to swim. She thought that the salt in the ocean water might have had something to do with her feeling.

Design an experiment to see whether Frances's guess was correct. Write your answers in the spaces provided. Include these elements in your response:

Hypothesis: _____

_____

_____

_____

Factor to be varied: _____

_____

Two factors to be held constant:

1 _____

2 _____

Procedure: _____

_____

_____

_____

_____

_____

_____

_____

Content Clue

The factor being tested here is *buoyancy*. If Frances felt lighter in the ocean, it was because she was more buoyant. The buoyancy of an object changes as the substance in which it is located changes.

Test Tip

Scientists can be influenced by what they already believe and by the opinions of others. Be aware of these factors when you write your **hypothesis** and design your **experiment**.

Practice

Forms of Energy

Eric bought a pair of sunglasses that didn't seem to work well. Other pairs lying around his house seemed to work better. He wondered whether certain types of lenses blocked out more sunlight than other types.

Design an experiment to see whether Eric's guess was correct. Write your answers in the spaces provided. Include these elements in your response:

Hypothesis: _____

_____

_____

_____

Factor to be varied: _____

_____

Two factors to be held constant:

1 _____

2 _____

Procedure: _____

_____

_____

_____

_____

_____

_____

_____

✏️ **Test Tip**

Be careful to test for only one **variable.**

📖 **Content Clue**

Lenses are all **convex** in shape but are made of different materials and different thicknesses. They may also have different types of coatings.

Practice

Forces and Motion

One day while Joyce's bicycle was being fixed, she borrowed her friend Mary's bicycle. As she rode Mary's bicycle, it seemed to her that it coasted better than her own bicycle did. She thought the reason might be that Mary's bicycle had smoother tires.

Design an experiment to see whether Joyce's guess was correct. Write your answers in the spaces provided. Include these elements in your response:

🖊 **Test Tip**

Coasting better might mean coasting farther, coasting faster, or both. You need to decide which of these two **variables** you are testing and provide a way to measure it.

Hypothesis: _____

_____

_____

_____

Factor to be varied: _____

_____

Two factors to be held constant:

1 _____

2 _____

Procedure: _____

_____

_____

_____

_____

_____

_____

_____

_____

_____

CHAPTER 8

Performing Science in the Laboratory

In the field of science, people learn by doing, either in the laboratory or out in the field. The Grade 8 Intermediate-Level Science Test includes a section that requires you to demonstrate your knowledge of skills used while working in a laboratory.

This chapter will give you some basic information to help you on the laboratory portion of the examination. In this chapter you will also learn about laboratory safety and how to use lab equipment to observe, measure, and classify data, and how to prepare lab reports.

Safety

When doing experiments, you must always be aware of proper safety procedures and possible safety hazards. You may sometimes work with materials or equipment that can be dangerous if not handled properly. Scientists consider safety in the lab to be important not only to themselves but also to their experiments. The following guidelines can help you avoid accidents in the laboratory. Here are the safety rules you will be required to follow:

- Plan your work.

- Follow the steps of an experiment in order.

- Never work alone in the laboratory.

- Never eat or drink anything in the laboratory.

- Keep your body safe.

- Be careful with electricity.

- Be careful handling laboratory equipment.

- Dispose of materials properly.

Plan your work. Always read about an experiment before beginning. Study the steps of the experiment so you know what to expect. If you have any questions, ask your teacher. Be sure you understand all safety symbols. Before beginning the experiment, clear your work area, including the aisles, of all items that won't be used.

Test Tip

When performing an **experiment,** follow all instructions exactly.

Safety Alert

Before you begin work in a lab, look for possible dangers, and prepare for them. For example, make sure there is a first-aid kit nearby.

Follow the steps of an experiment in order. Scientific experiments usually follow a logical order. Changing that order could cause unexpected reactions and safety problems. It could also ruin the results of the experiment.

Never work alone in the laboratory. If an accident happens, you will need someone to help you.

Never eat or drink anything in the laboratory. Chemicals or other materials you are working with can contaminate your food. Your food can also contaminate the experiment.

Keep your body safe. If you have long hair, tie it back so it does not get in the way. Roll or push up long sleeves. Wear protective clothing, such as gloves and an apron, when working with messy or dangerous materials. Cover any exposed cuts. If something spills onto a cut, wash that area immediately, and tell your teacher.

Wear safety goggles whenever you work with chemicals and other objects that could get into your eyes. If chemicals do get into your eyes, flush your eyes immediately with water, and tell your teacher.

Be careful with electricity. Check all electrical equipment for loose plugs or worn cords. Keep your hands dry around electricity. Water is a good conductor of electricity, so you can get shocked if your hands are wet. Also, make sure electric cords are in a safe place, where you cannot trip over them. Don't ever pull a plug from an outlet by its cord.

Be careful handling laboratory equipment. Check all glassware for chips or cracks before using it. Do not try to clean up broken glass. Instead, notify your teacher if glassware breaks. Air-dry all glass cups and other equipment. Do not use paper towels to dry them. Never use the palm of your hand to push glass tubing into the hole of a rubber stopper.

Be careful when using sharp objects, such as scissors and scalpels. Always dissect specimens in a dissecting pan. Never dissect a specimen while holding it in your hand. Always cut in the direction away from your body.

Safety Alert

Review with your teacher where the sink and a fire extinguisher are located and what procedures to follow in case of an accident.

Safety Alert

When using a liquid substance, make sure to recap its bottle after you have poured the needed amount.

Safety Alert

When you are done in the lab, put away all chemicals and lab tools. During your test, make sure that you put things back where and as you found them. Clean them if needed.

Dispose of materials properly. Dispose of materials as instructed by your teacher. When finished, always clean everything you used and clean your area.

Should there be an accident or should you or any members of your group get hurt, tell your teacher immediately.

Using Laboratory Equipment

Use these guidelines to help you handle the following lab equipment effectively.

Hand Lens In order to see objects magnified, hold the hand lens about 12 cm from your eye. Bring the object closer until it comes into focus.

Microscope Always carry a microscope with both hands. Avoid touching the lenses. Before you place a slide on the microscope stage, use the coarse-adjustment knob to raise the eyepiece as high as it will go. Then adjust the lenses so that you will be looking through the lens with the lowest power. This is usually the shortest lens. Place the slide on the stage. Then lower the lens so that it is close to the slide but not touching it. Focus by adjusting the lens slowly upward with the coarse-adjustment knob. When the slide is almost in focus, switch to focusing with the fine-adjustment knob. To use the high-power lens, first focus the slide under low power. Then move the higher-power lens into place.

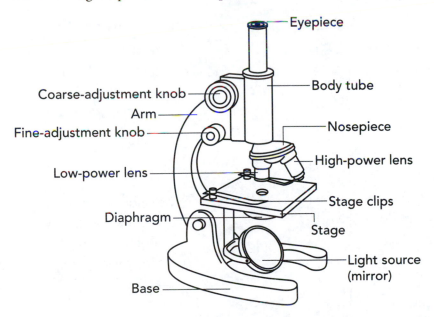

Which part of the microscope holds the slide in place? _____

> **Content Clue**
>
> Most **microscopes** used in school labs are optical microscopes. Optical microscopes use visible light to magnify objects. A glass **lens** or series of lenses focuses the light.

> **Test Tip**
>
> When using a microscope, be careful not to hit the slide when moving from low power to high power. If you are not paying attention, you could damage the slide or the microscope.

Ruler or Meter Stick To measure the length of an object, place the zero end of the ruler or meter stick next to one end of the object you are measuring. Next, find the other end of the object, and read the number next to it on the ruler or meter stick. This is the length of the object. Make sure to record the right units, such as centimeters (cm) or inches (in.).

Spring Scale Spring scales measure the force being exerted on an object. To measure the force of gravity (weight), attach the object to the hook on the spring scale, and slowly lift the scale. When the spring's motion stops, read the number the pointer is pointing to.

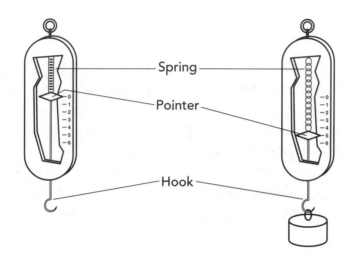

Spring

Pointer

Hook

What force is being measured by this spring scale? _____

Graduated Cylinder A graduated cylinder has a scale on the side marked in milliliters. It is usually used to measure the volume of a liquid.

Fill the graduated cylinder with liquid. Place it on a level surface with the measurement scale facing you. Move so that your eyes are even with the top of the liquid. You will notice that the surface of most liquids curves downward. This curve is called a *meniscus.* To correctly read the volume of a graduated cylinder, you must read the level of the liquid at the bottom of the meniscus.

What is the volume of the liquid in this graduated cylinder? _____

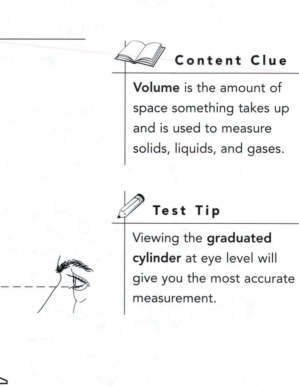

Triple-Beam Balance A triple-beam balance measures an object's mass by balancing it against three beams. On one side of the balance is a pan that holds the object. On the other side are three parallel beams with sliding masses. The numbers on the beams measure mass as the sliders move across the beams.

Before you put an object on the pan, make sure all three beam sliders are set to zero and that the pointer points to "0." To measure the mass of an object, place the object in the pan. Move the 100-g slider along the beam until the pointer drops below the fixed mark. Then move the slider back to the notch immediately to the left of this point. Follow the same procedure with the 10-g slider. The 1-g slider does not have notches, so you should move it back and forth until the beam balances. You can read this beam to the nearest tenth of a gram. To find an object's mass, add the numbers from all three beams.

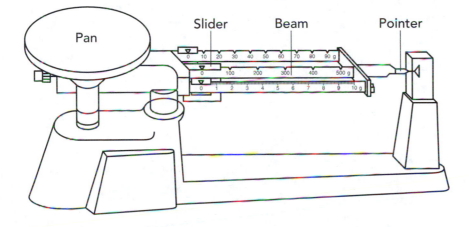

If the sliders are at 90, 200, and 3, what is the total mass of the object in the pan? _____

Thermometer Thermometers allow people to measure the temperature of the air, most liquids, and even our bodies. As the liquid in the tube of a thermometer gets warm, it expands and moves up the tube. It stops moving when it reaches the temperature of its surroundings.

To get the most accurate measurement, place the thermometer into the middle of the substance you are measuring. For example, if you are measuring the temperature of a cup of hot chocolate, place the thermometer in the middle of the cup. Scientists usually measure temperature in degrees Celsius, which is abbreviated °C.

 **Content Clue**

The most common kind of thermometer is the liquid thermometer. Most liquid thermometers have liquid mercury or alcohol inside a sealed glass tube. Some thermometers use a gas instead of a liquid.

Writing a Laboratory Report

As scientists perform experiments, they keep careful records of their observations and findings. They use these to create a lab report that sums up their experiment. A good lab report should be written clearly enough so that anyone reading it can duplicate the experiment. Include the following in your laboratory report:

Title The title of your report should be clear and specific. For example, an experiment comparing concave and convex lenses might be titled, "Comparing the Images Formed by Concave and Convex Lenses."

Purpose The purpose of a lab experiment is often put in the form of a question. A question might be, "What kinds of images are formed by concave and convex lenses?"

Hypothesis A hypothesis is a suggested solution to a problem or a possible explanation for why something happens. Before starting your experiment, you should state the hypothesis, or what you believe will be the results of the experiment.

Materials List all equipment used in the experiment. This will tell people what equipment they will need to repeat your experiment.

Procedure This section should include a step-by-step description of exactly what you did and the order in which you did it. Other people should be able to repeat your experiment by following your procedure. A diagram of the setup of the experiment would be helpful to include.

Observations Your observations should explain clearly what you saw during the experiment and list the data you gathered. Where appropriate, include tables, charts, graphs, or diagrams.

Conclusions Your conclusions should include an analysis of your data, written in paragraph form. Did your data support or reject your hypothesis? Your report may also include new questions to ask in order to get more support for your hypothesis.

Laboratory Practice

In the practices that follow, you will be given laboratory tasks at different stations and directions to follow. These lab practices will provide opportunities for you so that you can be successful on the laboratory section of the Grade 8 Intermediate-Level Science Test.

Content Clue

Experimental errors can cause unexpected results. Part of the experimental process is *error analysis*. Look at what was done. Did you follow the steps in the right order? Was something wrong with your equipment? This analysis should become part of your conclusions section of your laboratory report.

Test Tips

Keep a complete record of your observations, even those that do not seem important. They may become important later in the **experiment.**

Your conclusions should relate to the question you asked in the purpose section.

Check your laboratory report just as you would an essay. Look for mistakes in spelling, grammar, and punctuation.

Practice

Living and Nonliving Things

TASK: At this station, you will observe and draw two different types of cells. You will then use your drawings to identify the cells.

DIRECTIONS:

1 Place Slide A on the microscope stage. Bring it into focus using the lowest power. Now bring the slide into focus under the highest power. In the circle to the right, draw a typical cell on this slide under the highest power. Your drawing should accurately show the shape and structures of the cell. Label your drawing with the power you used.

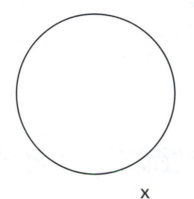

X _____

2 Place Slide B on the microscope stage. Bring it into focus using the lowest power. Now bring the slide into focus under the highest power. In the circle to the right, draw a typical cell on this slide under the highest power. Your drawing should accurately show the shape and structures of the cell. Label your drawing with the power you used.

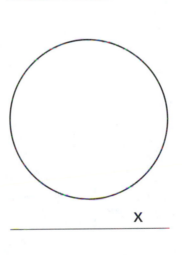

X _____

3 The cells on one slide are from plant tissue. The cells on the other slide are from animal tissue. Which slide do you think has cells from plant tissue? Why? _____

_____

_____

4 Compare Slides A and B. On a separate sheet of paper, describe any structures found in both and any other similarities. Also mention any differences.

Materials

Prepared slide of plant tissue, prepared slide of animal tissue (such as frog skin or frog blood), compound microscope with a low-power lens (about 100x magnification) and high-power lens (about 400x total magnification)

✏️ Test Tip

Draw in pencil so you can erase mistakes. Draw one structure at a time. Try to get that structure in the right proportion to the others.

✏️ Test Tip

Always mention the power of magnification when writing down results from using a **microscope**.

📖 Content Clue

Plant cells contain **chloroplasts** and rigid **cell walls**. Animal cells do not have either.

Practice

Genetic Information

TASK: At this station, you will model the transmission of genes for flower color in two generations of pea plants.

Materials

Basket A, filled with 16 pieces of purple poster board; Basket B, filled with 16 pieces of white poster board; 2 empty baskets, labeled C and D

DIRECTIONS:

1 The pieces of poster board represent genes for flower color in peas. Pull one gene from Basket A and one from Basket B. In Table 1, write the colors of the genes you picked. Put the genes in Basket C. Repeat this process, but this time put the genes in Basket D.

2 Repeat Step 1 until Baskets A and B are empty.

Table 1: First-Generation Plants			
1.	5.	9.	13.
2.	6.	10.	14.
3.	7.	11.	15.
4.	8.	12.	16.

Content Clue

In the tables, use *P* for purple and *w* for white.

3 In peas, purple flowers are dominant. White flowers are recessive. How many first-generation plants have purple flowers? _____ How many have white flowers? _____

4 Pull one gene from Basket C and one from Basket D. In Table 2, write the colors of the genes you picked. Repeat this process until Baskets C and D are empty.

Table 2: Second-Generation Plants			
1.	5.	9.	13.
2.	6.	10.	14.
3.	7.	11.	15.
4.	8.	12.	16.

5 How many second-generation plants have purple flowers? _____ How many have white flowers? _____

6 On a separate sheet of paper, tell what you can conclude about heredity from this experiment.

Practice

Change Over Time

TASK: At this station, you will observe fossils and compare them with organisms that exist today.

DIRECTIONS:

1 At this station there are *seven* fossil specimens, including those of a trilobite, a brachiopod, a fern, an echinoderm, a coral, a gastropod, and a cephalopod. The fossils are randomly labeled 1, 2, 3, 4, 5, 6, and 7. There are only *six* specimens of modern organisms, including a crayfish, a clam, a fern, a sand dollar, a coral, and a snail. They, too, are randomly labeled, as A, B, C, D, E, and F.

2 Examine the fossils carefully. Compare them with the modern organisms. In the table below, write the letter of the modern organism that most closely resembles each fossil specimen.

Fossil	Modern Organism	Fossil	Modern Organism
1		5	
2		6	
3		7	
4			

3 The cephalopod fossil is not related to any of the modern specimens included here. It is related to the modern squid and octopus. Which fossil specimen number was the cephalopod?

_____

4 Which two fossils most closely resemble their modern

counterparts? _____

5 Which two fossils look least like their modern counterparts?

_____

6 What can you infer from the existence of fossils millions of years old that closely resemble species that exist today? Write your answer on a separate sheet of paper.

 **Content Clue**

Trilobites are extinct arthropods whose bodies are divided into three segments. Brachiopods are marine **invertebrates** with shells like mollusks. Gastropods and cephalopods are mollusks.

> **Materials**
>
> **Fossil specimens:**
> Trilobite, brachiopod, fern, echinoderm, coral, gastropod, cephalopod
>
> **Modern specimens:**
> Crayfish, clam, fern, sand dollar, coral, snail

Practice

Reproduction and Development

TASK: At this station, you will observe through a microscope how yeast cells reproduce.

DIRECTIONS:

1 Measure 20 mL of warm water into the beaker. Then add 2 mL of corn syrup and 5 mL of dry yeast. Swirl the solution around gently, using a stirring rod.

2 Take a drop of the yeast culture you made from the beaker and place it on a microscope slide. Add one drop of methylene blue stain and carefully lower the cover slip.

3 Place the slide under the microscope and focus it under low power. Then focus it under high power. Observe the yeast cells. They should be reproducing.

4 Look for a yeast cell that has a bud on it. First, look for the cell wall. Then find the nucleus in the daughter cell. In the circle to the right, draw and label what you see.

5 Watch the yeast cells until you have seen one cell go through the entire budding process. Write a short paragraph that describes

what you saw.

_____

_____

_____

_____

6 Compare this type of reproduction to that of a frog.

_____

_____

Materials

Safety goggles, lab apron, pitcher of warm tap water, 250-mL beaker, corn syrup, packets of dry yeast, stirring rod, eyedropper, methylene blue stain, 100-mL graduated cylinder, 10-mL graduated cylinder, microscope slides, cover slips, microscope

Content Clues

Yeast is a type of **fungus** that is used to help make bread rise.

Budding is a form of **asexual reproduction.**

Test Tip

If you don't see any yeast **cells** reproducing, ask your teacher to look through the **microscope.** There might not be any yeast cells on your slide.

Content Clue

Animals use **sexual reproduction,** which requires two parents.

Practice

Meeting Daily Needs

TASK: At this station, you will test foods to see if they contain starch or protein.

DIRECTIONS:

1 Take a slice of potato, a slice of apple, and a tablespoon of breakfast cereal from their containers. Put them on a paper plate.

2 Fill a test tube about one-quarter full with milk. Fill a second test tube about one-quarter full with distilled water.

3 Put 3 or 4 drops of Lugol's solution on each piece of food and in each test tube. After 1 minute, observe the areas where you put the solution. Place a check mark in the starch column of the data table below Step 5 for each one that turned blue-black.

4 Measure 10 mL of Biuret solution and pour it into a test tube. Repeat until you have filled 5 test tubes with 10 mL each.

5 Add $\frac{1}{4}$ teaspoon pureed potato to the first test tube and shake the tube. Place a check in the protein column of the table below if the Biuret solution turns purple. Repeat with milk, pureed apple, breakfast cereal dissolved in water, and distilled water.

Food	Starch	Protein
Potato		
Milk		
Apple		
Breakfast cereal		
Distilled water		

6 Of the foods you tested, which contained the most protein?

_____

7 Of the foods you tested, which contained starch? _____
Name three other foods, not in this experiment, that would also

contain starch. _____

_____

Materials

Slice of potato, pureed potato, slice of apple, pureed apple, breakfast cereal, milk, paper plates, distilled water, test-tube rack, 7 test tubes, Lugol's solution, Biuret solution, eyedropper, set of measuring spoons

Safety Alert

Be careful not to let any chemicals or solutions used in **experiments** get on your skin. They can be harmful if touched or swallowed.

Content Clues

Lugol's solution is used to detect starch, which is another word for **carbohydrate.** In the presence of starch, Lugol's solution turns blue-black.

Biuret solution is used to detect **protein.** In the presence of protein, Biuret solution turns purple. The darker the purple color of the Biuret solution, the more protein it contains.

Practice

Energy in Ecosystems

TASK: At this station, you will test leaves for starch to find out if photosynthesis has occurred in them.

DIRECTIONS:

1 A geranium plant was kept in sunlight and watered. Four days before the experiment, half of the leaves were covered with aluminum foil. The day of the experiment, the leaves were cut from the plant and put in boxes. The box containing the covered leaves was labeled A. The other box was labeled B.

2 Take one leaf from the box labeled A and one leaf from the box labeled B. Remove the aluminum foil covering the leaf from box A. On a separate sheet of paper, describe what you see.

3 Place both leaves in the beaker and add 25 mL of alcohol. Place the beaker in the water bath. Gently heat the water bath on the hot plate for 5 minutes. *Do not touch the surface of the hot plate, and remember to turn the hot plate off when you are done.*

4 Using tongs, remove the beaker from the water bath. Describe below what happened to the alcohol and the leaves.

_____

_____

5 Place both leaves on a sheet of white paper. Using a dropper, cover them with Lugol's solution. Then wait 3–5 minutes.

6 Observe both leaves. Lugol's solution turns blue-black in the presence of starch. Describe or draw where starch was found in

each leaf. _____

_____

7 In photosynthesis, plants use light to combine carbon dioxide and water to make sugar. On a separate sheet of paper, draw a conclusion about the occurrence of photosynthesis in the leaves you tested.

Materials

Safety goggles, lab apron, 2 boxes of leaves, 100-mL beaker, 100-mL graduated cylinder, isopropyl alcohol, water bath, electric hot plate, Lugol's solution, eyedropper, white paper, timer

Test Tip

Always be careful to keep track of items that look alike but are treated differently during an **experiment.**

Safety Alert

Wear safety goggles when you do this experiment. Also, alcohol is extremely flammable. Use caution.

Content Clues

Plants store sugar as starch in their leaves. They later convert it to **glucose,** a simple sugar, for **energy.**

Practice

Humans and the Environment

TASK: At this station, you will measure the acidity (pH) of four different samples of water. You will then identify the samples based on the acidity you measure.

DIRECTIONS:

1 Pour water from the bottle labeled Sample 1 into the test tube labeled Sample 1. Pour enough water to fill half the test tube.

2 Repeat the procedure for the other samples.

3 Follow the directions on the pH indicator paper and measure the acidity of the sample in each test tube. Write your results in the table below.

Sample	pH
1	
2	
3	
4	

4 Acid rain has a pH value of between 2.0 and 5.0. Sample 4 is rain water collected from your area. Is it acid rain? Explain your answer.

_____

Which other sample is acidic enough to be acid rain? _____

5 Distilled water has a pH of 7.0. Which sample is distilled water?

_____

6 A lower pH means higher acidity. Sample 1 is tap water from your area. Which is more acidic, the local rain water or the local

tap water? _____

7 What factors could cause rain to become acidic? _____

_____

_____

Materials

4 bottles of water, labeled Sample 1, Sample 2, Sample 3, and Sample 4; pH indicator paper with instructions and indicator chart; 4 test tubes, labeled Sample 1, Sample 2, Sample 3, and Sample 4

Content Clue

The **pH scale** is used to measure acidity. The pH of a substance normally ranges from 1 to 14. A substance with a pH of 1 is extremely acidic. A substance with a pH of 14 is extremely basic. A substance with a pH of 7 is neutral.

Content Clue

You may be familiar with litmus paper, which can be used to tell if something is acidic or basic. The pH indicator paper also uses color to tell acidity. However, it is more exact than litmus paper.

Practice

The Earth and Space

TASK: At this station, you will draw what you observe first through one convex lens, then through two convex lenses used together.

DIRECTIONS:

1 Hold the styrofoam block with the convex lens in it so that the lens is at arm's length. Look out your window through the lens at a distant object, such as a tree in the yard. Move the styrofoam block closer or farther away from you, stopping when you see the object clearly through the lens.

2 In the circle to the right, draw the object as it appears through the one lens.

**Object through
one lens**

3 Without moving the first lens, hold a second convex lens close to your eye. Move the second lens back and forth slowly. Stop when you can see the distant object clearly through both lenses. Press the second lens into the styrofoam block.

4 Use the styrofoam block as a holder for the lenses. Hold the block in one hand, and with the other hand, in the circle to the right, draw the object as it appears through both lenses.

**Object through
two lenses**

5 On a separate sheet of paper, compare drawings. Describe the detail in each. Also mention any differences.

6 Also on this separate sheet of paper, describe what you would see on the Moon through a refracting telescope that you could not see with the naked eye. Explain your answer.

Materials

2 convex lenses, styrofoam block

 **Safety Alert**

Be careful to not focus on the Sun or any other light source with your **lenses**.

Test Tip

Be sure to look at the same object from the same position in both steps 1 and 4.

Content Clue

A lens is a piece of glass that refracts, or bends, light. **Convex lenses** are thicker in the middle than at the side. Convex lenses are used in **refracting telescopes,** the kind you are constructing here.

Practice

The Interaction of Air, Land, and Water

TASK: At this station, you will examine four different rocks and identify them.

DIRECTIONS:

1 Pick up each rock sample and look at it. Write its color in the table below.

2 Examine each rock sample with the hand lens. Look at the size of the grains. In the column labeled "Grain Size" in the table below, write *coarse, medium,* or *fine* for each rock. Next, look for crystal structures in each rock sample. For the column labeled "Crystals" in the table, decide whether crystals are present in each rock sample and write *Yes* or *No*.

3 Use sandpaper to scratch the surface of each rock sample slightly. With an eyedropper, put a drop or two of vinegar on the scratched area. In the table, write the reactions.

Rock	Color	Grain Size	Crystals	Reaction With Vinegar
1				
2				
3				
4				

4 Which sample is obsidian? _____

5 Which sample is limestone? _____

6 Which sample is granite? _____

7 Which sample is sandstone? _____

8 Wash each rock sample with distilled water and air dry on a towel.

Materials

Numbered rock samples, sandpaper, vinegar, eyedropper, towel, hand lens, distilled water

**Content Clues**

Fine grains look like small grains of sand. Coarse grains are lumpy.

Crystals are natural solids with a definite geometric shape. For example, table salt and iron have cube-shaped crystals.

**Content Clue**

Obsidian is a black, glassy-looking **igneous rock.** Limestone and sandstone are **sedimentary rocks** that do not have visible crystals. Granite is a coarse-grained igneous rock in which **mineral** crystals can be easily seen with a hand **lens.**

**Content Clue**

Limestone reacts with weak acids, such as vinegar, to form bubbles. Sandstone does not.

Practice

Physical Properties of Matter

TASK: At this station, you will measure the masses of empty and blown-up balloons. You will identify some variables that would affect the mass of the balloons. Then you will formulate a hypothesis.

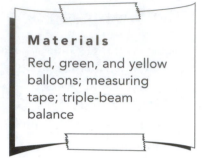

Materials

Red, green, and yellow balloons; measuring tape; triple-beam balance

DIRECTIONS:

1 Measure the masses of an empty red balloon, an empty green balloon, and an empty yellow balloon. Record the masses below.

red _____ green _____ yellow _____

2 Blow up each balloon so that its circumference is 35 cm. Use a tape measure or string to check the measurement. Tie the end of the balloon in a knot so no air can escape.

Content Clues

The circumference is the distance around the widest part of the balloon.

3 Measure the masses of the blown-up balloons and record the numbers below.

red _____ green _____ yellow _____

4 Why are the masses of the blown-up balloons different from the masses of the same balloons when empty? _____

_____

_____

Safety Alert

Make sure each person has his or her own balloons, to avoid the spreading of germs. Throw used balloons away.

5 Subtract the mass of each empty balloon from the mass of the same balloon when blown up. Record the numbers below.

red _____ green _____ yellow _____

What do these numbers give the mass of? _____

6 Cold air is denser than warm air. Write a hypothesis about how changing the temperature of the air used to fill a balloon will change the mass of the blown-up balloon. _____

_____

_____

Test Tip

Be very careful when taking measurements for question 5. Take them more than once. Even slight differences in measurements can be important to the results of an **experiment**.

Practice

Forms of Energy

TASK: At this station, you will use the appropriate materials to build an electrical circuit. You will then test the remaining materials to determine whether they are electrical conductors or insulators.

DIRECTIONS:

1 Examine the materials in the box. Choose the materials you need, and build a complete electrical circuit that will light a bulb. Include a switch in your circuit.

2 Draw a simple but accurate diagram in the box below, showing your completed circuit.

3 Test the five remaining materials in the box to see if they are electrical conductors or insulators. To do this, put each item, one at a time, in the space between the contact points of the switch. Make sure the item makes good contact with the components of the circuit. Record your results in the table below.

Material	Conductor or Insulator

4 On a separate sheet of paper, tell what type of circuit you built, a series or a parallel. Explain your answer.

Materials

Flashlight bulb, bulb holder, D cell battery, battery holder, 5 pieces of insulated wire, 1 large paper clip, 2 thumbtacks, 1 piece of plywood, chalk, glass, plastic spoon, metal spoon, wooden ruler, box

Safety Alert

Use caution when working with **electricity**. Keep hands off "live" wires.

Content Clues

An electrical **conductor** is a material that electricity can easily travel through. An electrical **insulator** is a material that does not conduct electricity easily.

The word *circuit* means "circle." An electrical **circuit** must provide a circle around which **electrical energy** can travel.

Practice

Forces and Motion

TASK: At this station, you will find out how the position of the fulcrum affects how a lever works.

DIRECTIONS:

1 Put the flat stick on the pencil so that the Line 1 mark is over the pencil as shown in the figure below. Place the two checkers on the stick as shown. Push gently on the other end of the stick. Measure how high the checkers were lifted. Record your measurements in the table below.

2 Repeat Step 1 with the fulcrum at Lines 2 and 3.

3 Write "easiest," "harder," and "hardest" in the table to describe the amount of force you had to use to raise the checkers.

Materials

Tape, pencil, flat stick, metric ruler, 2 checkers

📖 **Content Clue**

There are three classes of **levers:**

In a first-class lever, the **fulcrum** is between the **effort force** and the load.

In a second-class lever, the load is between the fulcrum and the effort force.

In a third-class lever, the effort force is between the fulcrum and the load.

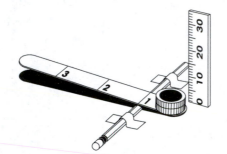

Fulcrum	Line 1	Line 2	Line 3
Height from table top to end of stick			
Force (easiest, harder, hardest)			

✏️ **Test Tip**

If necessary, repeat the experiment to help judge the force needed to raise the checkers.

4 On what line was the fulcrum when you moved the checkers the longest distance? _____ Where was the fulcrum when the least force was needed to move the checkers? _____

5 What can you conclude about how the position of the fulcrum affects how a lever works? _____

_____

Practice Test: Part A

The Living Environment

Directions (1–33): Each question is followed by four choices. Decide which choice is the best answer. Mark your answer in the spaces provided on the separate answer sheet by writing in the number of the answer you have chosen.

1 Which human body system moves oxygen into the blood and carbon dioxide out of the blood?

  1 skeletal

  2 respiratory

  3 digestive

  4 circulatory

2 The cell's chromosomes contain

  1 hereditary information

  2 reproductive cells

  3 cytoplasm

  4 pollen

3 The human system of circulation is similar to the plant system of

  1 photosynthesis

  2 transport

  3 reproduction

  4 respiration

Use the following diagram to answer Questions 4 and 5.

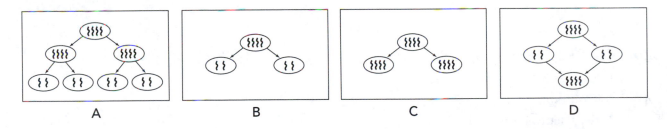

4 Which of the drawings above represents meiosis?

  1 A

  2 B

  3 C

  4 D

5 Which of the drawings on p. 143 represents mitosis?

   1 A

   2 B

   3 C

   4 D

6 Calories measure the amount of energy in

   1 oxygen

   2 electricity

   3 light

   4 food

7 Which of these nutrients are sources of energy for the body?

   1 carbohydrates and fats

   2 salt and water

   3 vitamins and minerals

   4 proteins and oxygen

8 Which of the following is an example of a fossil?

   1 DNA

   2 mutation

   3 footprint in rock

   4 living tree

9 All animals have which of the following?

   1 specialized cells

   2 jointed appendages

   3 lungs

   4 a backbone

10 Grouping organisms by their structures and origins is called what?

   1 biology

   2 evolution

   3 the scientific method

   4 classification

11 The brain, spinal cord, and neurons make up which body system?

   1 circulatory system

   2 nervous system

   3 support system

   4 reproductive system

12 Which part of the flower makes pollen?

   1 pistil

   2 ovary

   3 stamen

   4 pollen tube

The Physical Setting

13 The Sun seems to rise and set because of the Earth's

   1 revolution

   2 temperature

   3 rotation

   4 axis tilt

14 The thinnest layer of the Earth is the

   1 mantle

   2 crust

   3 lithosphere

   4 core

15 Sedimentary rock would be the most likely of all the rock types to contain

   1 fossils

   2 gemstones

   3 magma

   4 lava

16 How does heat cause rocks to metamorphize?

   1 It causes rocks to weather and erode.

   2 It makes rocks denser and heavier.

   3 It changes the chemical bonds of minerals.

   4 It causes particles to cling to each other.

17 Which of the following are examples of natural resources?

   1 oil and trees

   2 metals and minerals

   3 oceans and rivers

   4 all of the above

Use the following diagram to answer Question 18.

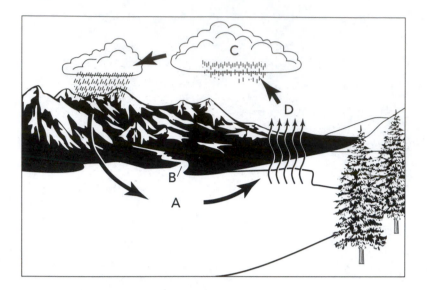

18 Which letter shows the process of evaporation?

1 A

2 B

3 C

4 D

19 What is the process that turns water into water vapor?

1 condensation

2 oxygenation

3 precipitation

4 evaporation

20 What type of object is the Sun?

1 a very large, gaseous planet

2 a galaxy

3 a star

4 a constellation

21 Every atom has the same number of protons as which of the following?

1 molecules

2 neutrons

3 electrons

4 neurons

22 Which of the following is an example of a physical change?

   1 sharpening a pencil

   2 cooking an egg

   3 a bicycle rusting

   4 milk turning sour

23 Usually, as a substance passes from a liquid phase to a solid phase, its molecules

   1 absorb heat energy and move farther apart

   2 absorb heat energy and move closer together

   3 release heat energy and move farther apart

   4 release heat energy and move closer together

24 How do we see an object, such as a baseball cap?

   1 The baseball cap absorbs all light.

   2 The baseball cap reflects light to our eyes.

   3 The baseball cap refracts light away from our eyes.

   4 The baseball cap neither absorbs nor reflects light.

25 What happens to electricity when an electrical circuit is open?

   1 It cannot flow.

   2 It becomes stronger.

   3 It changes direction.

   4 It moves in a circular path.

26 Liquid and gas are two phases of matter. What is the third phase?

   1 metal

   2 solid

   3 mineral

   4 ice

27 Which of the following is a good conductor of heat?

   1 metal

   2 wood

   3 rubber

   4 glass

28 Which of the following objects attract each other?

   1 two negatively charged objects

   2 two objects with opposite charges

   3 two positively charged objects

   4 two objects with no charge

29 What type of energy does a ball have as it rolls down a hill?

1 kinetic energy

2 nuclear energy

3 potential energy

4 light energy

30 Energy cannot be created nor destroyed. It can only do what?

1 change its weight

2 change its mass

3 change its form

4 change its density

31 Which of the following is an example of a force?

1 gravity

2 weight

3 inertia

4 motion

32 How many centimeters make up one inch?

1 1

2 2.5

3 20.5

4 4

33 What is the first step in any scientific investigation?

1 write a report

2 record your results

3 state the problem

4 run an experiment

Practice Test: Part B

The Living Environment

Directions (34–60): **For each question followed by four choices, decide which choice is the best answer. Mark your answer in the spaces provided on the separate answer sheet by writing the number of the answer you have chosen. For the remaining questions, write your answers in the space provided on the answer sheet.**

Base your answers to Questions 34–36 on the Punnett square and information below.

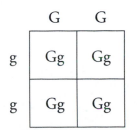

In plants, the gene for green pea pods (G) is dominant over the gene for yellow pea pods (g). The Punnett square shows the results of a cross between a pure green pea plant and a pure yellow pea plant.

34 What percentage of offspring are likely to be green pea plants?

35 On your separate answer sheet, show the probable results of crossing a hybrid green plant offspring with a pure yellow pea plant.

36 What do Punnett squares predict?
1 inherited traits
2 reproductive ability
3 photosynthesis
4 life span

Base your answers to Questions 37–41 on the photosynthesis diagram below and on your knowledge of science.

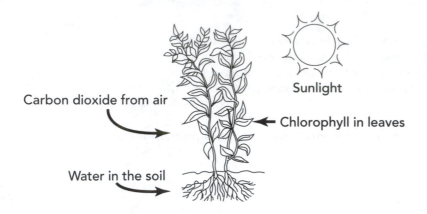

37   What is the energy source in this diagram?

38   What function does chlorophyll perform?

39   What is the gas given off by plants during photosynthesis?

40   How would a lack of sunlight affect photosynthesis?

41   Describe the process of photosynthesis.

Base your answers to Questions 42 and 43 on the diagram below, which shows a form of reproduction, and on your knowledge of science.

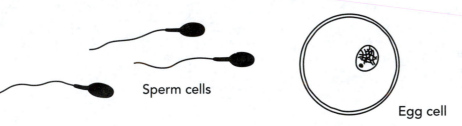

42   What kind of reproduction is shown in this diagram?

43   What happens when the sperm and egg join?

The Physical Setting

Use the table below to answer Questions 44–46.

Planet	Diameter (km)	Period of Rotation (in Earth days or Earth hours)	Period of Revolution (in Earth days or Earth years)
Mercury	4,900	58.7 days	88 days
Venus	12,000	243 days	225 days
Earth	12,750	24 hours	365.2 days
Mars	6,800	24 hours	687 days
Jupiter	143,000	9.8 hours	11.9 years
Saturn	121,000	10.2 hours	29.5 years
Uranus	51,000	17.9 hours	84 years
Neptune	49,000	19.1 hours	164.8 years
Pluto	2,300	6.4 days	247.7 years

44   The table above shows the diameters of the planets. Which statement is best supported by the data in the table?

1 Venus is larger than the Earth.

2 Mars is exactly half the size of Venus.

3 Jupiter is larger than all the other planets.

4 Uranus and Neptune combined are larger than Saturn.

45   Which statement about the planets is correct?

1 The largest planet also has the shortest rotation period.

2 The planet farthest from the Sun has the shortest period of revolution.

3 Venus and Mars have similar periods of rotation.

4 Jupiter's period of revolution is exactly twice as long as Neptune's.

46   Most asteroids are found in a belt between Mars and Jupiter. Which of the following is a reasonable inference about asteroids based on the data in the table?

1 Most asteroids are between 6,800 and 143,000 kilometers in diameter.

2 Asteroids are large chunks of rock.

3 Most asteroids probably have a rotation period similar to that of Mars.

4 Asteroids probably have a period of revolution that is between 687 days and 11.9 years.

Use the table below to answer Question 47. It shows the masses and volumes of a baseball, a basketball, and a golf ball. The formula for calculating an object's density is

$$\text{Density} = \frac{\text{Mass}}{\text{Volume}}$$

	Mass (g)	Volume (cm³)
Baseball	145	205.0
Basketball	567	7,400.0
Golf ball	45	40.5

47 Which statement about the densities of these objects is correct?

1 A basketball is denser than a baseball.

2 A golf ball is denser than a baseball.

3 A baseball is denser than a golf ball.

4 A baseball and a golf ball have equal densities.

48 Using the formula above for finding density, which statement about the volume is correct?

1 An object's volume depends on its mass.

2 If an object's volume increases, its density remains the same.

3 If an object's volume increases, its density decreases.

4 If an object's volume increases, its density increases.

Use the pie graph below to answer Question 49.

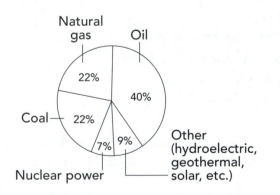

49 The pie graph above shows energy sources in the United States in recent years. Which kind of energy did the United States use the least?

1 nuclear power

2 hydroelectric, etc.

3 coal

4 natural gas

Wave A

Wave B

Wave C

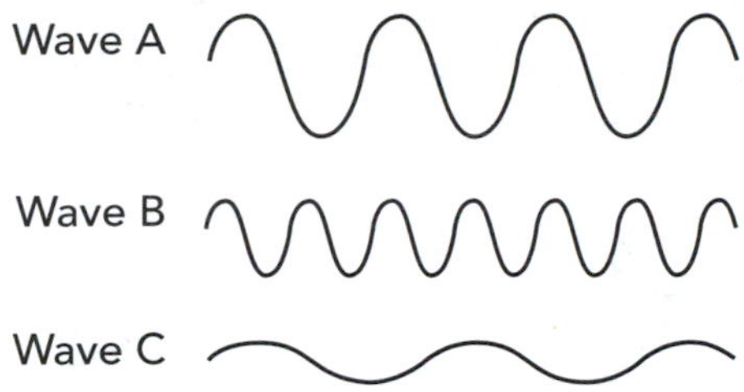

50 The diagram above shows three wavelengths. The longest wavelengths have the lowest frequencies. The shortest wavelengths have the highest frequencies. Which statement is best supported by the diagram?

1 Wave A has a higher frequency than Wave B.

2 Wave B has a longer wavelength than Wave A.

3 Wave A has a longer wavelength than Wave C.

4 Wave A has a higher frequency than Wave C.

51 Light travels in waves. Infrared light has a wavelength that is too long to see. If the three wavelengths shown are light, which is most likely to be infrared light?

52 Which of the three waves has the most energy?

53 Sound also travels in waves. Low frequency sound waves are also low in pitch. Which of the three waves has the highest pitch?

Base your answers to Questions 54–56 on the diagram below and on your knowledge of science.

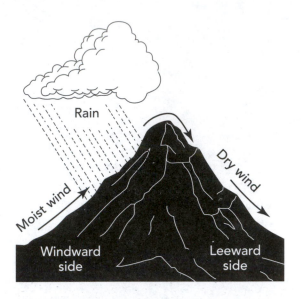

54 Explain why the climate on the windward side of the mountain is usually wet and rainy.

55 Which characteristic of the mountain might allow some moist, warm air to flow over the top and fall on the leeward side?

56 As it is forced over the mountain, an air mass becomes cooler and denser. Predict what will happen to the air mass on the leeward side of the mountain.

Base your answers to Questions 57–60 on the diagram below, which shows lines of longitude and latitude on a globe.

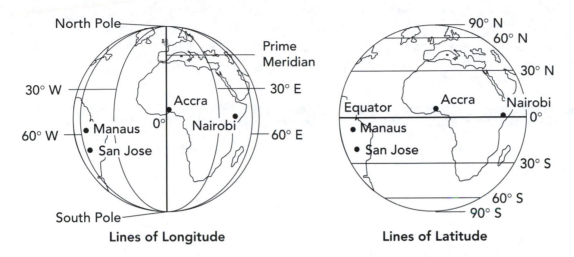

Lines of Longitude   Lines of Latitude

57   Which lines are continuously the same distance apart, lines of latitude or lines of longitude?

58   What city in the diagram is closest to the equator?

59   At what degree of latitude is the North Pole?

60   At what two points do all the lines of longitude meet?

Practice Test: Part C

The Living Environment

Base your answers to Questions 61–63 on the graphs below. They show the growth of two plants that are both provided with adequate light and water but grown in *separate* containers.

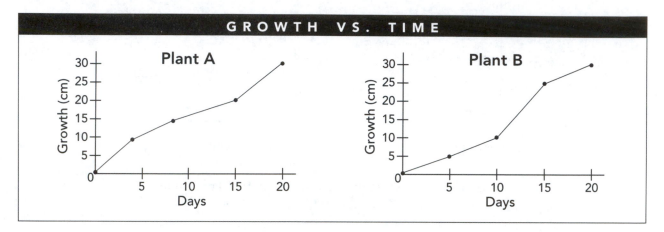

61 The data below were obtained when Plant A and Plant B were grown in the *same container* and given adequate light and water.

Day	Growth				
	0	5	10	15	20
Plant A	3 cm	5 cm	7 cm	8 cm	8 cm
Plant B	3 cm	6 cm	9 cm	11 cm	13 cm

On the grid provided on your separate answer sheet, make a graph of the data from the table above according to the instructions below.

a Place an *X* to show the growth of Plant A for each interval in the 20-day period.

b Connect the *X*s with a *dashed* line.

c Place a dot in a circle to show the growth in Plant B for each interval in the 20-day period.

d Connect the circled dots with a *solid* line.

62 State the relationship that may have produced the results shown when Plant A and Plant B were grown together in the *same container,* as opposed to when Plant A and Plant B are grown in *separate containers.* Explain your answer, using the graphed data.

63 Based on your graph, predict the growth of Plant A or Plant B at Day 21. Explain your prediction.

The Physical Setting

Base your answers to Questions 64 and 65 on the chart below, which lists substances and their densities.

Substance	Density (g/cm²)
Hydrogen gas	0.00009
Air	0.001
Gasoline	0.66
Water	1.00
Milk	1.028

64 According to the chart above, which of the substances is likely to rise in air?

65 According to the chart above, which of the liquid substances will most likely float on water?

Base your answers to Questions 66 and 67 on the diagrams below, which show the Moon in two different positions in relation to the Earth.

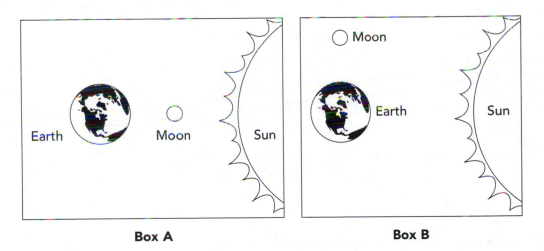

Box A   **Box B**

66 Looking at the Moon from the Earth as shown in Box A, in what phase is the Moon?

67 How much time has probably elapsed between Box A and Box B?

68 A student notices that the Sun feels much hotter when she is wearing a black T-shirt than when she is wearing a white T-shirt. She wonders if it might be because light is absorbed by a black surface and reflected by a white surface. Design an experiment to see if her hypothesis is correct. Include these elements in your response:

- State the hypothesis.
- Identify the factor to be varied.
- Identify two factors that should be held constant.
- Clearly describe the procedure.

Base your answers to Questions 69–71 on the information below, the map on p. 159, and on your knowledge of science. The notes below were made by a student doing a research project about weather patterns in the continental United States.

Some Observations About a Weather Map

1 The temperatures in the southern part of the United States are warmer than the temperatures in the northern part.

2 There are several different types of weather occurring at the same time in the United States.

3 Weather systems generally move from west to east.

Background Information Found in Science Book

1 An air mass is a huge body of air that moves from place to place.

2 A front is the place where two air masses of different temperatures meet.

3 A cold front occurs when a cold air mass moves against a warm air mass, forcing the warm air upward. The rising warm air cools quickly, causing short, but heavy, rain or snow. The temperatures drop as the cold front passes.

4 A warm front occurs when a warm air mass moves into and slides over a cold air mass. The warm air cools as it rises along a gentle slope, resulting in precipitation that is light and long.

5 Low pressure refers to areas where the air pressure is low. This generally means rainy or stormy weather. Almost all storms occur in low-pressure areas.

---

69 In the space provided on your separate answer sheet, explain what kind of front is approaching Milwaukee, which direction it is moving, and what effect it will have on the weather there.

70 What do you expect the weather will be like soon in New York City? Explain the reasons for your prediction.

71 Is it warmer in Kansas City or in Pittsburgh?

Practice Test: Part D

This part of the test contains science performance tasks located at three different stations, labeled X, Y, and Z. During this test of lab skills, you will visit all three stations and do some different things at each station. You may already be seated at one of these stations. Use the materials at the station to help you do the tasks.

At each station you will have 15 minutes to complete your work. Continue working until you see the word *STOP* at the bottom of the page or until the 15 minutes are up. If you have extra time, check your work or wait quietly.

Do not help other students or ask others to help you. Everyone should work alone. There must be no talking between students during the test.

Read the directions for each station carefully. All of your answers must be recorded on the test pages.

After you complete the tasks at each station, prepare to leave the station. Please leave the station the way it is shown on the Station Diagram, which should be located on the lower left corner of the station or posted nearby.

Do not go on to the next page until you are instructed to do so.

Station X: Modeling Digestion

TASK: At this station, you will model the digestive action of saliva in the mouth by attempting to dissolve three different foods in water. Then you will model the action of enzymes that digest fats in the small intestine by adding baking soda to the water. Finally, you will compare your observations to the digestion that takes place in the mouth and in the small intestine.

DIRECTIONS:

1   Read all directions for this activity before you begin your work.

2   Using a wax pencil, label one test tube *sugar,* another *starch,* and the third *oil.* Put the test tubes in a test-tube rack.

3   Using the graduated cylinder, pour 5 mL of water into each test tube.

4   Put a pinch of sugar into the test tube labeled *sugar* and a pinch of starch into the test tube labeled *starch.* With an eye dropper, put 5 drops of oil in the test tube labeled *oil.*

5   Place a stopper in the top of one of the test tubes. Place your thumb over the stopper and shake the test tube for 30 seconds.

6   Observe the contents of the test tube immediately after shaking it. Record in the table the appearance of the liquid.

7   Repeat Steps 5 and 6 for the other two test tubes.

Data Table			
Test Tube	After Shaking	After 2 Minutes	After Adding Baking Soda and Shaking
Sugar			
Starch			
Oil			

8   Let the test tubes sit undisturbed for 2 minutes. Then record in the table the appearance of the liquid in each test tube.

9   After each test tube was shaken for 30 seconds, which substance or substances seemed to dissolve? _____

_____

10   Were any of the substances still dissolved in the water after 2 minutes?

If so, which ones? _____

_____

_____

11   Remove the stoppers, and add $\frac{1}{4}$ teaspoon of baking soda to all three test tubes. Replace stoppers and shake each test tube for 30 seconds. Record your observations in the data table.

12   Compare the different dissolving actions you observed to the digestion that takes place first in the mouth and then in the small intestine.

_____

_____

_____

_____

_____

After you have finished this activity, return the equipment to the positions shown in the Station Diagram.

Station Y: Experimenting with Blocks

TASK: At this station, you will measure the forces acting on a block and calculate the areas of the different surfaces of the block. You will then graph your findings.

DIRECTIONS:

1   With the ruler, measure the length and width of Side A of Block 1. Record your measurements in Table 1. Repeat for Sides B and C of Block 1.

2   The area of each side of Block 1 can be calculated by multiplying the length of each side by its width. Calculate the area of each side of Block 1. Record your results in Table 1.

3   Repeat Steps 1 and 2 with Block 2.

Table 1							
Block 1	**Length**	**Width**	**Area**	**Block 2**	**Length**	**Width**	**Area**
Side A				Side A			
Side B				Side B			
Side C				Side C			

4   Hook the spring scale to the short side of Block 1 and measure the weight of the block. Record your measurement in Table 2, on the next page.

5   Keeping the spring scale hooked, put Side B of the block on the table. Pull gently on the spring scale until the block just starts to move. Note the measurement on the spring scale and record it in Table 2.

6   Rotate the block so Side C of the block is flat on the table. Again, pull gently on the spring scale until the block just starts to move. Note the measurement on the spring scale and record it in Table 2.

7   Remove the spring scale and hook it to the long side of Block 1. Put Side A of the block flat on the table. Pull gently on the spring scale until the block just starts to move. Note the measurement on the spring scale and record it in Table 2.

8   Repeat Steps 5–8 with Block 2.

Table 2						
Block 1	**Weight:**			**Block 2**	**Weight:**	
	Force	**Area**			**Force**	**Area**
Side A				Side A		
Side B				Side B		
Side C				Side C		

9 From Table 1, enter on Table 2 the areas that you calculated for the sides of the blocks. Graph your results below. Be sure to include the units of scale on each axis of the graph.

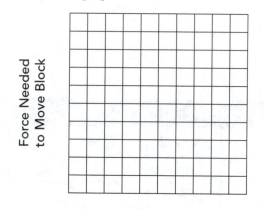

Area of Sides

10 Name the four forces acting on a block as it is pulled across the table.

1 _____   3 _____

2 _____   4 _____

11 Write a statement describing the relationship between the area of the side of a block lying flat on the table and the force needed to start the block moving. _____

_____

12 Write a statement describing the relationship between the weight of a block and the force needed to start the block moving. _____

_____

After you have finished this activity, return the equipment to the positions shown in the Station Diagram.

Station Z: Minerals

TASK: At this station, you will test minerals for various properties and use your results to identify the minerals.

DIRECTIONS:

1   Rub each mineral sample on the tile streak plate. Note the color the streak produced. Record your results in Table 1 below. Write *none* if the mineral does not make a streak. Note that some minerals have a white streak, the same color as the tile.

2   Scratch each sample with your fingernail. If your fingernail can scratch the mineral, it has a hardness of less than 2.5. Record this in Table 1.

3   Use a penny to try to scratch each sample that your fingernail could not scratch. If the penny can scratch the mineral but your fingernail could not, the mineral has a hardness of between 2.5 and 3.5. Record your results in Table 1.

4   Use the piece of glass to scratch each sample that the penny could not scratch. If the glass can scratch the mineral but the penny cannot, the mineral has a hardness of between 3.5 and 6. If the glass cannot scratch the mineral, it has a hardness of greater than 6. Record your results in Table 1.

5   Use the eye dropper to place a drop or two of acid (vinegar) on each mineral sample. Observe each reaction and record it in Table 1.

6   Put the magnet next to each sample. Record the reaction in Table 1.

Table 1				
Sample No.	Streak	Evaluation of Hardness	Reaction to Acid	Reaction to Magnet
1				
2				
3				
4				
5				
6				
7				
8				

Table 2	
Sample No.	Mineral
1	
2	
3	
4	
5	
6	
7	
8	

7 Use the following information to identify the mineral samples. Record your results in Table 2 above. If you have trouble, try scratching one mineral with another to determine which of the two is harder.

- Barite has a hardness of 3 to $3\frac{1}{2}$. Its streak is white, and it does not react to vinegar or to a magnet.
- Calcite has a hardness of 3. Its streak is white/gray. Calcite bubbles in vinegar but does not react to a magnet.
- Fluorite has a hardness of 4. Its streak is white, and it does not react to vinegar or to a magnet.
- Graphite has a hardness of 1 to 2. Its streak is gray/black, and it does not react to vinegar or to a magnet.
- Magnetite has a hardness of $5\frac{1}{2}$ to $6\frac{1}{2}$. Its streak is black. Magnetite does not react to vinegar, but it is attracted to a magnet.
- Pyrite has a hardness of 6 to $6\frac{1}{2}$. Its streak is green/black. Pyrite does not react to vinegar, but it is attracted to a magnet.
- Quartz has a hardness of 7. It produces no streak, nor does it react to vinegar or to a magnet.
- Talc has a hardness of 1. Its streak is white, and it does not react to vinegar or to a magnet.

After you have finished this activity, return the equipment to the positions shown in the Station Diagram.

Glossary

The following list includes all the words that appear in the Vocabulary boxes found in Chapter 1, "Reviewing the Content." It also includes other scientific terms or concepts you might be required to know for the examination or for a general understanding of science. The page numbers that follow indicate where in Chapter 1 the word or words can be found.

acceleration (ak-sel-uh-RAY-shun) change in an object's speed or direction

acid chemical compound that reacts with a base to form a salt; acids release hydrogen when dissolved in water

acid rain rainwater containing nitric acid or sulfuric acid, p. 17

adaptation (ad-up-TAY-shun) trait of a living thing that makes it more able to survive in its environment and produce offspring, p. 8

air mass large area of air that has the same temperature and amount of moisture

alga a plantlike protist (plural, *algae*)

amino acid a building block of proteins

ampere unit used to measure electrical current

amphibian (am-FIB-ee-un) animal that lives part of its life in water and part on land

amplitude (AM-pluh-tood) height of a wave

anemometer (an-uh-MOM-uh-tur) instrument used to measure wind speed

antibody substance the body makes to protect itself from disease

anticline upward fold in rock layers

apogee (AP-uh-jee) point of the Moon's orbit at which the Moon is farthest from the Earth

appendage a part that extends out from an organism's body, such as a wing or an arm

artery a blood vessel that carries blood away from the heart

asexual reproduction type of reproduction needing only one parent, p. 6

asteroid large chunk of rock that orbits the Sun between Mars and Jupiter, p. 18

astronomical unit unit of measure equal to about 150 million kilometers, the distance from the Earth to the Sun

astronomy study of stars, planets, and other objects in space

atmosphere (AT-muhs-feer) thin layer of gases surrounding the Earth, p. 20

atom smallest part of an element that can be identified as part of that element, p. 22

atomic mass total mass of the protons and neutrons in an atom, measured in atomic mass units

atomic number the number of protons in the nucleus of an atom

axis imaginary line through the center of a planet, pole to pole, on which the planet rotates, p. 19

axon fiber that carries messages away from a nerve cell

bacterium single-celled organism that belongs to the Moneran Kingdom (plural, *bacteria*)

barometer instrument used to measure air pressure

base substance that reacts with an acid to form a salt; formed when metals react with water

battery series of electrochemical cells connected together

bedrock solid rock that lies beneath the soil

behavior ways in which living things respond to stimuli

biology the study of all organisms on Earth, including plants and animals

biome (BY-ohm) large region of the Earth with a particular climate and characteristic plant and animal life

blood vessel a tube that carries blood throughout the body

boiling point temperature at which a liquid changes to a gas

botany the study of plant life

bronchus (BRAHN-kus) one of two tubes leading to the lungs (plural, *bronchi*)

budding a type of asexual reproduction used by fungi and some plants; in budding a bulge is created in the organism that eventually separates and becomes a fully independent new organism, p. 10

calcium a mineral found in teeth and bone

calorie unit of heat; amount of heat needed to raise the temperature of 1 gram of water 1 degree Celcius; also, as the kilocalorie, or Calorie, unit used to measure energy from foods, p. 13

cancer disease resulting from abnormal cell growth

capacity (kuh-PAS-ih-tee) amount of material something can hold

capillary (KAP-uh-ler-ee) tiny blood vessel that connects an artery to a vein

carbohydrate (kahr-buh-HY-drayt) nutrient consisting of stored sugar or starch, p. 13

carbon dioxide gas made of molecules of carbon and oxygen released as a byproduct by animals and other organisms during respiration

carnivore consumer that eats only meat, p. 13

cell basic unit of structure and function in living things, p. 4

cell membrane thin, porous, wall-like structure that surrounds a cell, p. 4

cellular respiration the process cells use to release energy from food molecules, p. 4

cell wall rigid outer covering of a plant cell, p. 4

Celsius (SEL-see-us) metric scale used to measure temperature; unit used is degrees Celsius

Cenozoic era the geological era that began 65 million years ago

centripetal force a force that causes objects in motion to move in a curved path

cerebellum (ser-uh-BELL-um) part of the brain that controls balance and body motion

cerebrum (suh-REE-brum) large part of the brain that controls the senses and thinking

chemical bond a bond that holds molecules together

chemical change change that produces a new substance, p. 23

chemical energy energy stored in molecules, p. 24

chemical symbol abbreviation used for the name of an element

chemistry study of what matter is made of and how it reacts when it comes in contact with other matter

chlorophyll (KLOR-uh-fil) green material in chloroplasts that captures sunlight; needed by plants to carry out the chemical process of photosynthesis, p. 4

chloroplast organelle of green plant cells containing the green material chlorophyll, used to carry out photosynthesis, p. 4

cholesterol a substance found in some fats and also in the body; needed by the body in small amounts

chromosome (KROH-muh-sohm) threadlike structure in the nucleus of a cell that controls hereditary information, p. 6

circuit an unbroken circular path that an electrical current flows through; includes a source of energy, such as a battery, p. 25

circuit breaker switch that opens a circuit if too much current is flowing

circulation (sur-kyuh-LAY-shun) movement of blood through the body

circulatory system the body system that controls circulation of blood through the body and the exchange of gases, p. 5

cirrus (SIR-us) **cloud** light, feathery cloud

classification (biological) grouping organisms according to similar characteristics, such as internal and external structures, p. 5

climate average weather conditions in an area over a long period of time

cold-blooded having a body temperature that changes with the temperature of the environment

cold front forward edge of a cold air mass, formed when a cold air mass pushes under a warm air mass

colon a part of the large intestine; organ in the digestive system

comet body made up of rock, dust, gases, and ice that orbits the Sun, p. 18

community all the populations that live in a certain place at a certain time, p. 16

competition struggle to get a share of common resources, such as food and living space, p. 8

compound substance made up of two or more elements that are chemically combined, p. 23

compound machine machine that combines two or more simple machines, p. 27

condensation changing of a gas to a liquid, p. 21

conduction movement of heat through a solid

conductivity a measure of how easily a material will allow electricity or heat to flow through it, p. 22

conductor material that allows electricity or heat to flow through it easily, p. 25

conservation wise use of natural resources, p. 16

constellation (kon-stuh-LAY-shun) grouping of stars that form a pattern or picture in the sky

consumer (kun-SOO-mur) organism that obtains food by eating other organisms, p. 13

continent a very large landmass

continental drift theory that the continents were once a giant landmass that broke into pieces and moved around, eventually arriving at the positions they are in today

continental shelf part of a continent that slopes gently away from the shoreline into the water

continental slope part of a continent that lies between the continental shelf and the ocean floor

contour (KON-toor) **line** line on a map that connects all points having the same elevation

control part of an experiment in which the factor to be varied (variable) is not changed

controlled experiment a two-part experiment in which both experimental procedures are exactly alike except for one thing

convection (kon-VEK-shun) movement of heat through a liquid or a gas

convection current movement of a liquid or gas caused by changes in temperature; also, up and down movement of gases or liquids caused by heat transfer

convex (kon-VEKS) **lens** lens made of glass or plastic that is thicker in the middle than at the edges and curves outward

core solid, inner layer of the Earth; also, center of the Sun

cornea (KOR-nee-uh) clear covering at the front of the eye

corona (kuh-ROH-nuh) outer layer of the Sun's atmosphere

corrosion wearing away of a metal

crater (KRAY-tur) funnel-shaped pit at the top of a volcanic cone; also, round depression on a planet's or moon's surface

crescent (KRES-ent) **phase** phase when less than half the Moon or other body is visible in space

crest highest point of a wave

crust thin, solid, outer layer of the Earth, p. 20

crystal (KRIS-tul) a natural solid with a definite geometric shape

cumulonimbus cloud a tall, thick, white cumulus cloud that is dark at the bottom; also known as a thunderhead

cumulus cloud big, fluffy, low-lying, white cloud that usually signals good weather

current movement of water in the ocean or large body of water brought on by temperature differences, winds, and the Coriolis effect, among other things; electrical current refers to the flow of electrons through a conductor, p. 25

cycle something that happens over and over in the same way

cyclone an area of low pressure with circling winds

cytoplasm (SYT-uh-plaz-um) jelly-like, watery substance inside a cell that surrounds the nucleus and in which various organelles float, p. 4

data information

decibel unit used to measure the loudness of a sound

decomposer (dee-kum-POHZ-er) organism that breaks down the wastes or remains of dead organisms and absorbs nutrients from them, p. 13

density (DEN-sih-tee) amount of matter in a given volume, p. 22

density current ocean current caused by cold, salty water, which is very dense and sinks below warmer water

deposition (dep-uh-ZISH-un) process by which material carried by erosion is deposited, or dropped, in new places

dew point temperature to which water in the air must be cooled to reach saturation

digestion (di-JES-chun) process of breaking down food into forms that can be used by living things, p. 12

digestive system body system that breaks down food, chemically and physically, so that the body can use it for energy, growth, and repair; organs in the system include the mouth, esophagus, stomach, and intestines, p. 5

direct current current in which the electrons always flow in the same direction

disease any malfunction of a body organ or system due to infection or other natural causes, such as heredity, p. 5

dissolve to go into solution; to seem to disappear, p. 22

diversity variety of species due to the biological processes of evolution and mutation, p. 8

DNA molecule found in chromosomes that contains hereditary information, p. 7

dominant trait trait that always shows itself in organisms, p. 7

earthquake sudden, strong movement of the Earth's crust, p. 21

earth science the study of the Earth, including its rocks, oceans, air, and weather; also, the study of the Sun, Moon, planets, and stars

ebb tide outgoing, or falling, tide

echo reflected sound waves

eclipse passing of one planetary body through the shadow of another, p. 19

ecological succession gradual changes in an environment over many generations, p. 16

ecology study of the relationships between living things and their nonliving environments

ecosystem all the living and nonliving things in a particular environment, such as a pond or a fallen log, p. 14

effort force force applied when doing work, p. 27

egg female reproductive, or sex, cell, p. 6

electrical energy energy in the form of electrons moving through a substance, p. 25

electricity (i-lek-TRIS-uh-tee) form of energy caused by the movement of electrons from one substance to another

electromagnet temporary magnet made by wrapping a current-carrying wire around an iron core

electromagnetic spectrum complete range of different types of radiation, divided by either frequency or wavelength, p. 25

electromagnetism state that occurs when electricity and magnetism interact, forming a temporary magnet

electron atomic particle with a negative electrical charge, p. 25

element matter that is made up of only one kind of atom, p. 22

elevation distance above or below sea level

elliptical shaped like a flattened circle, or oval, p. 19

embryo organism in an early stage of development; in humans, this is the first three months in the life of an unborn baby, p. 11

emulsion (i-MUL-shun) suspension of two liquids

endangered living things that are in danger of dying out, or becoming extinct, p. 8

endocrine system body system that transmits chemical messages throughout the body, p. 5

energy ability to do work or produce heat; comes in various forms, such as heat energy, electrical energy, and light energy, p. 12

energy pyramid chart that shows how energy is lost as it moves through a community, p. 15

environment everything that surrounds a living thing, p. 8

enzyme (EN-zime) protein released by the body that controls chemical activities

epidermis (ep-uh-DUR-mis) dead outer layer of the skin; serves as protection for deeper layers

equator imaginary line that circles the Earth halfway between the North and South poles, p. 19

equinox (EE-kwuh-nahks) "equal night"; day on which the Sun shines directly on the equator

era largest division of geological time

erosion process by which rock or soil is worn away and moved to another place, p. 17

evaporate to turn into a gas, p. 23

evaporation changing of a liquid to a gas at the surface of the liquid, p. 21

evolution biological process by which organisms change over time due to natural selection and other influences, p. 9

excretion removal of waste products from the body, p. 13

excretory system body system that disposes of waste; also, the system that removes excess heat from the body, p. 5

experiment something that is done to test a hypothesis or prediction

extinct describes a species that no longer contains any living organisms, p. 8

extinction the disappearance of all living organisms in a species

fat a nutrient in foods that supplies the body with energy, p. 13

fault break in the Earth's crust along which movement has occurred

fertilization union of a male reproductive cell and a female reproductive cell to form a zygote, p. 6

fetus (FEET-us) term given to a developing baby before birth

filtration separation of particles in a suspension by passing it through paper or other substances

First Law of Motion physical law first stated by Sir Isaac Newton; says that an object in motion stays in motion and an object at rest stays at rest unless another force acts on it; also called the Law of Inertia, p. 26

focus place inside the Earth where an earthquake starts

food chain model for showing the flow of food energy from one organism to the next in a community, p. 14

food web way of showing how different food chains are related, p. 15

force any push or pull, p. 18

fossil remains or traces of an organism that lived millions of years ago, p. 9

fossil fuel fuel such as coal, oil, or gas that comes from the remains of once-living things, p. 24

freezing change of state from a liquid to a solid

freezing point temperature at which a liquid becomes a solid

frequency number of complete waves passing a point in a given time

friction force that opposes the motion of an object, p. 26

front boundary between two different air masses

fulcrum (FUL-krum) support on which a lever turns, p. 27

fungus (FUN-gus) plantlike organism that lacks chlorophyll; includes mushrooms, yeasts, and molds

fuse wire that melts and breaks a circuit if too much current is flowing; used to prevent fires

fusion process in which atomic nuclei combine to form new atoms; source of energy from the Sun, p. 22

galaxy very large group of stars that travel together through space

gamete reproductive, or sex, cell, such as sperm and egg

gas phase or state of matter that has no definite shape or volume

gene segment of DNA that contains one unit of hereditary information, p. 7

generator device that changes mechanical energy into electrical energy

genetic engineering set of methods used to change an organism's DNA, p. 7

genetics the study of heredity

genus biological classification group made up of related species

geological era a huge period of time in the Earth's history

geologic time scale division of the Earth's history based on types of organisms that lived at different times

geothermal energy energy produced from hot rocks deep inside the Earth, p. 25

germination the process by which a tiny new plant breaks through the hard seed coat protecting it

geyser (GY-zur) heated groundwater that erupts onto the Earth's surface

gibbous (GIB-us) **phase** phase when more than half the Moon or another body is visible in space

gill structure that produces mushroom spores; also, organ in fish that absorbs dissolved oxygen from water

glacier (GLAY-shur) slow-moving river of ice and snow, p. 21

gland organ that makes chemical substances used or released by the body, p. 5

global warming trend toward higher temperatures on the Earth's surface; in modern times, may be caused by an increased greenhouse effect, due to human activities such as the release of certain gases by cars, p. 17

global wind large wind system that moves around the Earth

globe spherical model of the Earth, p. 19

glucose a simple sugar that is made by producers and stored as a carbohydrate, p. 12

gram basic metric unit of mass

gravity force of attraction that exists between all objects in the universe; gravitational pull is determined by a body's mass and its distance from the object it is pulling on, p. 18

greenhouse effect process by which certain gases, such as carbon dioxide and water vapor, collect in the Earth's atmosphere and trap heat from the Sun, p. 20

groundwater water that collects in pores in the soil

habitat place where an organism lives

half-life length of time it takes for one-half the amount of a radioactive element to change into another element

heat total amount of energy in moving particles of a sample of matter

heat energy energy in the form of moving molecules, p. 24

hemoglobin (HEE-moh-gloh-bin) iron compound in red blood cells

herbivore consumer that eats only plants, p. 13

heredity the passing of genes and the traits they carry from parents to offspring, p. 7

hibernation (hy-bur-NAY-shun) inactive state of some animals during winter months

homeostasis (hoh-mee-oh-STAY-sis) the state of a living thing in which it keeps conditions inside its body constant even when the environment changes, p. 13

hormone chemical substance that regulates body functions, p. 5

host an animal that supports a parasite

humidity amount of water vapor in the air

hurricane tropical Atlantic storm with very strong winds

hybrid having two unlike genes in a pair of genes that control a certain hereditary trait; also, the offspring of parents of two different species

hybridization (hy-brid-ih-ZAY-shun) crossbreeding of organisms to produce offspring with new characteristics; often done on purpose by humans to produce improved traits in plants and food animals

hydroelectric energy form of electrical energy produced by moving water, p. 25

hydrometer (hy-DRAHM-uh-tuhr) device used to measure specific gravity

hydrosphere part of the Earth that is water, p. 21

hypothesis (hy-PAHTH-uh-sis) suggested answer or solution to a problem

igneous (IG-nee-us) **rock** rock that forms from magma, or molten rock beneath the Earth's surface, p. 20

immune system body system made up of cells and tissues that help an organism fight disease, p. 5

immunity (im-MYOON-i-tee) resistance to a specific disease

inclined plane simple machine made up of a slanted surface or ramp, p. 27

inert (in-URT) **gases** six elements that make up the last group in the Periodic Table of Elements

inertia (in-UR-shuh) tendency of an object to stay at rest or in motion unless acted on by an external force, p. 26

inference an explanation for what is observed; helps scientists to draw conclusions when doing experiments

infrared light part of the electromagnetic spectrum; an invisible light or type of radiation usually felt as heat, p. 25

insoluble (in-SAHL-yoo-bul) substance not able to be dissolved

insulator substance that does not conduct heat or electricity easily; material that prevents electrical charges from flowing through it easily

invertebrate (in-VUR-tuh-brayt) animal without a backbone

involuntary muscle muscle that causes movements that you cannot consciously control, for example, cardiac muscle; also called **smooth muscle**

ion (EYE-ahn) an atom with an electrical charge

ionization (Y-ahn-uh-ZAY-shun) the process that results in the forming of ions

ionosphere (y-AHN-uh-sfeer) upper layer of the Earth's atmosphere

isobar (EYE-suh-bar) line on a weather map that connects points of equal air pressure

isotope (EYE-suh-taupe) atom of an element with the same number of protons but an unusual number of neutrons

joint place where two or more bones meet

joule (JOOL) metric unit of work equal to 1 newton-meter

kilogram (KIL-uh-gram) 1,000 grams; metric unit of mass

kinetic (ki-NET-ik) **energy** energy of motion, p. 24

kingdom the most general level of biological classification, made up of related phyla, p. 5

landform physical feature of the Earth's surface

larva wormlike stage of insect development

laser device that produces a powerful beam of light

latitude imaginary line that circles the globe east to west; lines of latitude are measured in degrees north and south of the equator, which is 0 degrees latitude; aids in navigation

lava magma that reaches the Earth's surface

Law of Conservation of Energy law that states that energy cannot be made or destroyed, only changed in form

Law of Conservation of Mass law that states that during an ordinary chemical reaction, matter cannot be created or destroyed; its atoms can only be rearranged, p. 23

lens piece of curved glass that causes light rays to come together or spread apart as they pass through; part of the eye that forms an image on the retina; transparent material that bends light

lever simple machine made of a bar or rod that turns on a support, p. 27

life cycle predictable physical changes an organism experiences during its lifetime, from infancy to adulthood, p. 11

ligament tissue that connects bone to bone

light energy energy in the form of moving waves; made up of particles called *photons*, p. 24

light year distance light travels in a year, a unit of measurement equal to about 10 trillion kilometers

liquid phase or state of matter with a definite volume but no definite shape

liter basic metric unit of volume

lithosphere solid part of the Earth, p. 20

longitude imaginary line that circles the globe north to south; lines of longitude are measured in degrees east and west of the prime meridian, which is 0 degrees longitude; aids in navigation

lubricant substance that reduces friction, p. 26

luster the way a mineral reflects light from its surface; shine

machine a tool or device that makes work easier to do, p. 27

magma molten, or melted, rock inside the Earth

magnet piece of metal that attracts iron or steel; has north and south poles, p. 26

magnetic field area around a magnet where magnetic forces can act

magnetism natural force that occurs when objects made out of iron or steel are attracted by a magnet; force of attraction or repulsion, p. 26

magnitude (MAG-nuh-tood) measure of a star's brightness

mammal a warm-blooded vertebrate that has hair on its body; the mother's body makes milk to feed its young

mantle middle layer of the Earth, usually divided into upper mantle and lower mantle; upper portion contains rock that is like thick molasses and moves slowly

map flat model of the Earth

mass amount of matter in an object, p. 22

matter anything that has mass and volume or takes up space, p. 22

mechanical advantage number of times a machine multiplies the effort force

mechanical energy energy in the form of parts moving in a machine, p. 24

medulla (muh-DULL-uh) part of the brain that controls heartbeat and breathing rate

meiosis (my-OH-sis) cell division that produces sex cells, p. 6

melting point temperature at which a solid changes to a liquid

meniscus (mi-NIS-kus) curved surface of a liquid in a graduated cylinder

mesosphere the third layer of the Earth's atmosphere

Mesozoic era the geologic era that started about 240 million years ago and ended about 65 million years ago

metabolism sum of all the chemical reactions of the body, p. 13

metal element that has certain physical properties, such as hardness and shine, and can be melted and formed into shapes

metamorphic (met-uh-MOR-fik) **rock** rock that forms when existing rocks are changed into new types of rock by great heat and pressure, p. 20

metamorphosis (met-uh-MORE-fuh-sis) extreme physical changes during the stages of development of an organism; frogs and insects undergo metamorphosis, p. 11

meteor (MEE-tee-or) piece of rock, metal, or rock-metal combination that enters the Earth's atmosphere and burns up, p. 19

meteorite (MEE-tee-or-ite) piece of rock, metal, or rock-metal combination that reaches the Earth's surface without burning up, p. 19

meteoroid (MEE-tee-or-oyd) any piece of rock, metal, or rock-metal combination that orbits the Sun, p. 18

meteorology the scientific study of the Earth's weather and atmosphere

meter basic metric unit of length

microscope tool that makes things look larger than they really are, p. 4

microscopic too small to be seen by the naked human eye

mid-ocean ridge underwater mountain chain

migration (my-GRAY-shun) movement of animals from one living place to another far away, usually to find food or warmth

Milky Way the name of the spiral-shaped galaxy that contains the solar system

mineral nutrient needed by the body to develop properly; also, natural solid formed from elements and compounds in the Earth's crust, p. 13

mitochondria (myt-uh-KAHN-dree-uh) rice-shaped structures that produce energy for a cell, p. 4

mitosis nuclear cell division that results in two identical "daughter" cells with the same number of chromosomes as the parent cell; a type of asexual reproduction, p. 6

mixture two or more substances that have been put together but not chemically combined, p. 23

molecule (MAHL-uh-kyool) smallest part of a substance that has all the properties of that substance, p. 22

moneran tiny organism that has DNA but no true nucleus

moon a large, natural satellite of a planet, p. 18

motion change in the position of an object

multicellular containing more than one cell

muscular system body system that allows movement, p. 5

mutation change in an organism's DNA, p. 8

natural resource material, such as water and soil, found in nature that is used by living things, p. 16

natural selection process that gives organisms with favorable traits a better chance of surviving and producing offspring, p. 8

nebula (NEB-you-luh) cloud of hot gases found in space; birthplace of stars

nervous system body system that receives information from the environment and sends messages around the body, p. 5

neuron (NOOR-ahn) nerve cell

neutral having neither a positive nor a negative electrical charge; also, describes a substance that is neither acidic nor basic

neutron atomic particle with neither a negative nor a positive electrical charge

newton metric unit of force equal to one kilogram-meter per second

niche (NICH) organism's role, or job, in its habitat

nonrenewable resource natural resource that cannot be renewed or replaced in a reasonable amount of time, p. 17

nova star in which the outer layer has been blown off in an explosion

nuclear (NEW-klee-ar) **energy** energy released from the breaking apart or combining of atoms, p. 24

nuclear fission the breaking apart of atoms to release energy; used for the commercial generation of electricity, p. 24

nucleus (NEW-klee-us) control center of a cell; also, center, or core, of an atom, p. 4

nutrient (NOO-tree-unt) chemical substance in food needed by the body for energy, growth, and other life processes, p. 12

ocean basin bottom of the ocean floor

oceanography study of the Earth's oceans

offspring new organism produced by living things during either sexual or asexual reproduction, p. 6

omnivore a consumer that eats both plants and animals, p. 13

opaque (oh-PAYK) material that blocks most of the light hitting it, p. 25

orbit closed, curved path of one object around another object in space, p. 18

ore rock or mineral from which a useful metal can be removed; mineral that is mined because it contains useful metals or other substances

organ group of tissues that work together to do a special job, p. 4

organelle small structure in a cell's cytoplasm that does a special job, p. 4

organic compound chemical compound containing the element carbon; all known life forms are made of organic compounds

organism (OR-guh-niz-um) any living thing, including plants, animals, bacteria, and fungi, p. 4

osmosis (ahs-MOH-sis) movement of water through a membrane

ovary organ of the female reproductive system; also, the lower part of a flower's pistil

ovulation (oh-view-LAY-shun) release of a mature egg from the ovary

ovule (OH-vyool) part of a plant's ovary that contains an egg that develops into a seed after fertilization

oxygen gaseous element used by animals during respiration; it releases energy stored in foods

ozone layer layer of the atmosphere that protects the Earth from the Sun's harmful radiation, p. 17

paleontology study of fossils

parallel circuit circuit in which an electrical current can follow more than one path

parasite an organism that lives on or inside of another organism, called a host, and causes harm to its host

particulate tiny piece of soot or dirt that pollutes the air, p. 17

pedigree chart diagram that shows the genetic history of an individual, p. 7

perigee (PER-uh-jee) point at which the Moon is closest to the Earth

perihelion (per-uh-HEEL-yun) that point in a planet's orbit at which it is closest to the Sun

Periodic Table of the Elements chart showing all the known elements on Earth, arranged in groups that share certain characteristics; the chart contains important information about the elements, such as atomic number and mass, p. 22

petal special kind of plant leaf that is often brightly colored or scented to attract pollinators

phase a state of matter: solid, liquid, or gas; also, the way an object in space appears to us at a certain time of the month, due to its position relative to the Sun, p. 19

pH scale number scale used to measure acidity

phloem (FLOH-em) tissue that carries food made by a plant's leaves throughout the plant

photon (FOH-tahn) tiny bundle of light energy

photosynthesis (foht-uh-SIN-thuh-sis) food-making process in leaves that uses sunlight, water, carbon dioxide, and a material called chlorophyll found in chloroplasts in green plants; the food is a simple sugar called glucose, and it is stored in the plant as a carbohydrate, p. 12

phylum (FY-luhm) biological classification group made up of related classes; one level below kingdom

physical change change that does not produce a new substance and can be undone by various methods, such as filtration, p. 23

physical science the study of matter and energy

physics the study of what energy is and how it interacts with matter

pistil female reproductive organ in a flower, p. 11

pitch how high or low a sound is

plankton tiny organisms that drift in oceans or lakes; the beginning of many food chains in the ocean

plasma (PLAZ-muh) liquid part of blood

plate large chunk of the Earth's crust that fits together with other chunks, like pieces of a jigsaw puzzle; also called *tectonic plate*

platelet (PLAYT-lit) part of the blood that helps stop the bleeding caused by injuries

plate tectonics (tek-TAHN-iks) theory that states the Earth's crust is broken into plates that float or drift around on the Earth's mantle

pole one end of a magnet; also, one of the two furthest points, north and south, from the equator

pollen grain that contains a male plant reproductive cell

pollination (pahl-uh-NAY-shun) transfer of pollen from a plant's stamen to a pistil, often by animals such as insects or bats, p. 11

pollutant any substance that upsets the balance of an ecosystem, p. 17

pollution the state of being polluted by harmful materials; some types of pollution are air and water pollution, p. 7

population group of the same kind of organism living in a certain place at a certain time, p. 16

pore tiny opening; hole or air space

potential energy stored energy, p. 24

power amount of work done per unit of time

Precambrian era the longest geologic era; it started 4 billion years ago, shortly after the Earth is thought to have been formed, and lasted about 4 billion years

precipitation (prih-sip-uh-TAY-shun) water that falls to the Earth from the atmosphere, p. 21

predator consumer who hunts, kills, and eats other live animals for food, p. 15

pressure force per unit area

prey animal eaten by a consumer who is a predator, p. 15

primary consumer a consumer who eats only plants, p. 15

prism (PRIZ-um) triangular 3-dimensional piece of clear glass that breaks up white light into a band of colors known as a spectrum

producer (pruh-DOOS-ur) organism that makes its own food, using sunlight or chemical energy, p. 13

product substance that is formed in a chemical reaction, p. 23

property (PRAHP-ur-tee) feature that is used to help describe an object

protein (PRO-teen) nutrient needed to build and repair cells, p. 13

protist (PROHT-ist) single-celled organism that has a nucleus

proton atomic particle with a positive electrical charge

protozoan (proh-tuh-ZOH-un) one-celled, animal-like protist; an amoeba is an example

pulley simple machine that is a rope wrapped around a wheel with grooves, p. 27

Punnett square chart that shows possible gene combinations, p. 7

pupa (PYOO-puh) stage of complete metamorphosis in which an insect spins a protective covering around itself

pupil opening in the center of an eye's iris

radiation (ray-dee-AY-shun) movement of energy through space in the form of waves

radioactive giving off radiation, or harmful rays

radioactive dating a way to find the age of rocks by measuring the decay, or breakdown, of radioactive elements in them

radio telescope telescope that can receive radio waves from sources in space

reactant material used in a chemical reaction, p. 23

recessive trait trait that is hidden when a dominant gene is present, p. 7

recycle to use a natural resource over and over again, p. 17

red blood cell blood cell that carries oxygen

red giant large, bright star that is fairly cool

reflecting telescope telescope that uses mirrors to collect light

reflection bouncing back of a light wave after striking a barrier, p. 25

reflex automatic response by an organism to a stimulus

refracting (rih-FRAKT-ing) **telescope** telescope that uses convex lenses to produce an enlarged image

refraction bending of a light wave as it moves from one medium to another, p. 25

relative (REL-uh-tiv) **humidity** amount of water vapor in the air compared to the total amount of water vapor the air can hold

renewable resource natural resource that can be renewed or replaced in a reasonable amount of time, p. 16

reproduction process by which living things produce new organisms like themselves

resistance opposition to the flow of an electrical current

resistance force any force, such as gravity, that opposes the effort force, p. 27

resistor material that opposes the flow of an electrical current, p. 25

resource something useful to organisms; natural resources are resources from nature, p. 8

respiration process of carrying oxygen to cells, getting rid of carbon dioxide, and releasing energy; process by which living things combine oxygen with food molecules to produce energy, p. 12

respiratory system body system that takes in oxygen from air and passes it into the bloodstream, p. 5

response (ri-SPAHNS) an organism's reaction to a change or a stimulus

revolution one complete movement of a planet or other body in its orbit, p. 19

Richter (RIK-ter) **scale** scale that measures the energy released by an earthquake

rift valley deep crack running down the center of the mid-Atlantic ridge

Ring of Fire major earthquake and volcanic zone that almost forms a circle in the Pacific Ocean

rock cycle series of natural processes by which rocks are slowly recycled, or changed, from one kind of rock into another kind, p. 20

rotation (roh-TAY-shun) spinning of a body on its axis; rotation produces the day-night cycle on Earth, p. 19

runoff rainwater that flows into streams and rivers

salinity (suh-LIN-uh-tee) amount of dissolved salts in ocean water

saliva liquid substance in the mouth that aids in digestion

satellite natural or artificial object orbiting a body in space

saturated solution solution containing all the solute it can hold at a given temperature

scale feature that relates distances on a map to actual distances on the Earth

scavenger animal that eats only dead organisms

scientific method model, or guide, used to gather information and solve problems

screw a simple machine that is an inclined plane wrapped around a cylinder, p. 27

sea-floor spreading process in which hot magma from inside the Earth is pushed upward, creating new sea floor material, p. 21

secondary consumer a consumer that eats primary consumers, p. 15

Second Law of Motion law first stated by Sir Isaac Newton that a force acting on an object causes the object to accelerate, or speed up, in the direction of the force; acceleration will be in direct proportion to the force and inverse proportion to the object's mass, p. 26

sediment (SED-uh-munt) soil and rock particles that, through erosion and decomposition, can form into sedimentary rock

sedimentary rock rock that forms from deposits of particles of other rocks or the remains of once-living things; often contains fossils, p. 8

seed structure that contains a tiny living plant and food for its growth

seed coat protective outside covering of a seed

seismic (SIZE-mik) **wave** earthquake wave

seismograph (SIZE-muh-graf) instrument that detects and measures earthquakes

series circuit circuit in which the electrical current follows along only one path

sexual (SEK-shoo-wul) **reproduction** the creation of new offspring by the combining of genes from two parents, p. 6

simple machine machine that accomplishes work, usually in one motion, p. 27

skeletal system the internal supporting structure of an organism, made up mostly of bones and cartilage, p. 5

smog mixture of smoke, fog, and chemicals

smooth muscle see **involuntary muscle**

soil rocks on the Earth's surface broken down by weathering to very tiny pieces that mix with the nutrients from living and nonliving things, p. 17

solar eclipse passing of the Moon between the Earth and the Sun, forming a shadow on the Sun

solar energy sunlight used as an energy source, p. 24

solar system the Sun and all the bodies that revolve around it, including planets, moons, asteroids, and other objects, p. 18

solid phase or state of matter with a definite shape and volume

solstice (SOHL-stis) "Sun stop"; day on which the North Pole points toward or away from the Sun, depending on whether it is summer or winter

solubility the ability of a substance to be dissolved into another substance, p. 22

soluble (SAHL-yoo-bul) describes a substance able to be dissolved in a solution

solution mixture in which one substance is evenly mixed with another substance, p. 23

sonar a type of tracking system that bounces sound waves off the ocean floor (*sound navigation ranging*); used for locating objects

sound vibrations that travel in waves through solids, liquids, or gases

species (SPEE-sheez) group of organisms that share certain important characteristics and can reproduce among themselves, p. 5

specific gravity density of a substance compared with the density of water

spectroscope (SPEK-truh-skohp) instrument that separates light into different colors

spectrum band of the different colors of light, p. 25

speed distance traveled per unit of time

sperm male reproductive, or sex, cell, p. 6

spore small body that detaches itself from the parent organism during asexual reproduction to produce new offspring, p. 10

spring tide tide that is higher or lower than normal tides

stamen (STAY-mun) male reproductive organ in a flower, p. 11

star large ball of glowing gases that gives off light and heat, p. 18

state of matter also called *phase,* the way a substance is usually found; the common states of matter are solid, liquid, and gas, p. 22

stigma (STIG-muh) top part of a pistil on a flower

stimulus and response something that causes a reaction to take place in an organism and (response) the organism's reaction to that stimulus, p. 13

stoma tiny opening in the underside of a leaf that allows the exchange of gases

stratosphere (STRAT-uh-sfeer) the second layer of the Earth's atmosphere, where the ozone layer is found

stratus cloud low-lying, gray cloud that covers a large area

streak color of the powder left by rubbing a mineral against a hard surface

striated (STRY-ayt-ed) **muscle** muscle attached to the skeleton, making movement possible; also called *voluntary muscle*

subduction (sub-DUKT-shun) **zone** place on the Earth's surface where old crust is pushed down into a trench

substance any element or compound

sunspot dark, cool area on the Sun's surface

supergiant very large star

supernova very large star that has been blown apart in a violent explosion

supersaturated solution solution containing more of a dissolved substance than it can normally hold at a given temperature

suspension (suh-SPEN-shun) cloudy mixture of two or more substances that settle on standing

system a group of organs working together in an organism to perform an important function, p. 4

technology science discoveries and skills put to use in practical ways

temperature measure of how hot or cold something is; measure of the average kinetic energy of the particles in a substance

tendon (TEN-dun) tissue that connects muscle to bone

tertiary consumer consumer that eats secondary consumers, p. 15

theory (THEE-uh-ree) idea that explains something and is supported by data

thermal pollution damage that occurs when waste heat enters the environment

thermosphere the fourth layer of the Earth's atmosphere

Third Law of Motion law first stated by Sir Isaac Newton that for every force applied to an object, there is an equal and opposite reaction force, p. 26

tide the rise and fall of the Earth's oceans, caused by the gravitational pull of the Sun and Moon

tissue group of similar cells that work together, often forming an organ, p. 4

tornado small, very violent, funnel-shaped storm

trait characteristic of an organism, often produced by heredity, p. 6

translucent describes a material that transmits some light, p. 25

transparent describes a material that transmits most of the light hitting it, p. 25

transpiration process by which plants give off water vapor into the air

transport the carrying of materials and nutrients throughout an organism using that organism's circulatory system, p. 12

trench long, V-shaped valley on the ocean floor

tropical zone warm region near the equator

tropism growth of a plant in response to something in the environment

troposphere (TROHP-oh-sfeer) lowest layer of the Earth's atmosphere, where weather takes place

trough (TROFF) lowest point of a wave

tsunami (tsooh-NAH-mee) ocean wave caused by an earthquake; also called a *seismic sea wave*

turbine a machine with blades that can be turned; used to start an electrical generator

ultraviolet light radiation with very short wavelengths that cannot be seen by the human eye; causes tanning in skin and can cause sunburn and skin cancer; most ultraviolet rays are screened out by the ozone layer of the Earth's atmosphere, p. 25

unicellular containing only one cell

unit amount used to measure something

universe all that exists, including the Sun, Moon, stars, planets, and space

uplifting and folding a geological process that bends layers of the Earth's crust and sometimes turns them upside down, p. 21

urine liquid waste formed in the kidneys

uterus (YOOT-ur-us) organ in which an embryo develops

vacuole (VAK-yoo-wohl) storage area in the cytoplasm of a cell

vacuum almost totally empty space, lacking even air or gas molecules

variable anything that can be changed in an experiment

variation differences in traits among individuals of a species, p. 8

vein tube that contains the xylem or phloem in a leaf; also, blood vessel that carries blood to the heart

velocity (vuh-LAHS-u-tee) speed and direction of motion

vent opening in a volcano from which magma flows

vertebrate (VUR-tuh-brate) animal with a backbone

vibration rapid back-and-forth movement of air or an object, p. 25

virus a very small disease-causing particle that is mostly DNA

visible light seven colors that make up white light in the electromagnetic spectrum, p. 25

vitamin nutrient found naturally in tiny amounts in many foods, p. 13

volcano opening or vent in the Earth's crust from which magma, rock, and gases are emitted; also, the pile of volcanic material around the vent, p. 21

volt unit used to measure the force of an electrical current or the stored power of a battery

volume amount of space something takes up

voluntary muscle muscle that can be controlled; also called **striated muscle**

warm-blooded having a body temperature that remains about the same, whatever the surroundings

warm front forward edge of a warm air mass

water cycle continuous movement of water between the Earth's surface and the atmosphere, p. 21

wave regular up-and-down movement of water; also, a disturbance that transfers energy from place to place

wavelength distance between two neighboring wave crests or troughs, p. 25

weather day-to-day conditions of the Earth's atmosphere, p. 20

weathering a process that breaks down rocks and minerals; can be caused by wind, water, or ice, p. 20

wedge simple machine made of two inclined planes, back to back, p. 27

weight measure of the pull of gravity on an object

wheel and axle simple machine that consists of a wheel attached to a rod called an axle; as the axle turns, the wheel also turns, p. 27

white blood cell blood cell that fights off bacteria and helps protect the body against disease

white dwarf very small, hot star

wind horizontal movement of air

work what happens when a force moves something through a distance; force times distance, p. 27

xylem (ZY-lum) tissue that carries water and dissolved minerals upward from the roots of plants

zoology the study of animal life

zygote (ZY-gote) cell formed by fertilization in sexual reproduction; through cell division, the zygote will develop into an embryo, p. 6

Index

A
acceleration, 108
acid rain, 15, 36, 87
adaptations, 6, 7
analyzing, 77
anther, 9, 49
asexual reproduction, 4, 8, 32, 66, 67, 134
asteroids, 16, 17, 88
atmosphere, 18, 19, 38
atom, 20, 21, 55, 75, 79, 91, 96
atomic mass, 55
atomic number, 55
axis, 17, 29, 37

B
bacteria, 3, 4, 64
binary fission, 4, 8
biomes, 52
Biuret solution, 135
blood, 2, 3
blood vessels, 3, 64
budding, 8, 134

C
calories, 11, 34, 106
carbohydrates, 11, 68, 101
carbon dioxide, 18, 46, 69, 87, 103, 118, 136
carbon dioxide-oxygen cycle, 69
carnivores, 11, 50
cell membrane, 1, 2, 97
cells, 2, 3, 5, 58, 131
cellular respiration, 2, 10, 11
cell wall, 2, 8, 30, 81, 97, 131
Celsius scale, 43, 77, 129
characteristic, 5
charts, 93, 94, 96, 100, 104, 105, 106
chemical change, 21, 39, 111
chemical energy, 22, 91
chlorophyll, 2, 46, 81, 97
chloroplasts, 2, 12, 30, 46, 97, 131
chromosomes, 4, 5, 31, 33, 62, 63, 65, 66, 98
circuits, 23, 56, 141
circulatory system, 3, 64
classification, 3, 79, 81
classifying, 78, 79, 90
climate, 18
comets, 16, 17
commensalism, 70
community, 14, 70
comparing, 78
compound, 21
compound machine, 25
condensation, 19, 54
conduction, 40, 60
conductors, 23
conservation, 14
consumers, 11, 12, 79, 86, 102, 118
control group, 110
convection, 40, 60
currents, 23
cytoplasm, 2, 5, 8, 30, 64, 97

D
decomposers, 11, 13, 34, 86, 102
density, 20, 39, 72
diagrams, 42, 43, 44, 45, 46, 48, 49, 50, 51, 52, 53, 54, 55, 56, 57, 67, 69, 75, 79, 84, 90, 91, 92, 141
digestion, 10
digestive system, 3
disease, 3
DNA, 4, 5, 62, 63, 65

E
Earth, 16, 17, 18, 19, 29, 37, 41, 53, 60, 71, 72, 79, 88, 92, 104
earthquake, 19, 38, 105
eclipse, 17, 76
ecological succession, 14
ecology, 87
ecosystem, 12, 14, 35, 36, 66, 69, 70, 102
effect, 80
effort force, 25
egg, 4, 5, 8, 9, 33, 49
electrical energy, 23, 56, 141
electromagnetic spectrum, 23
electrons, 23, 55
elements, 20
embryo, 9, 100
endangered, 6
endocrine system, 3
energy, 10, 22, 68, 69, 121
energy pyramid, 13, 35, 69
environment, 6, 32
equator, 17
erosion, 15, 19
evaporation, 19, 21, 54
evolution, 7, 61
excretion, 11
excretory system, 3
experiment, 109, 110, 111, 112, 113, 114, 115, 116, 117, 118, 119, 120, 121, 122, 123, 124, 125, 126, 136
experimental group, 110
extinct, 6, 32
extinction, 6

F
fact, 80
fats, 11, 68, 101
fertilization, 4, 5, 8, 9, 33
fertilizers, 117, 119
filament, 9, 49
filtration, 21
food chain, 12, 13, 102
Food Guide Pyramid, 11
food web, 13, 102
force, 24, 41, 92, 108, 142
fossil fuels, 22, 70
fossils, 7, 32, 48, 133
friction, 24, 75
fulcrum, 25, 142
fungus, 3, 30, 34

G
gametes, 67
gas, 20, 21, 38, 60, 128, 129

genes, 5, 65, 98, 132
genetic engineering, 5
geothermal energy, 23
glaciers, 19
glands, 3
global warming, 15
globe, 17
glucose, 10, 136
graduated cylinder, 128
gram, 77
graphs, 93, 95, 96, 99, 103, 105, 106, 108
gravity, 16, 24, 25, 37, 92
greenhouse effect, 18, 87

H, I
hand lens, 127
heart, 2, 3
heat energy, 22, 54, 56, 91
herbivores, 11, 13, 50
heredity, 5
homeostasis, 11
hormones, 3
horse, 7
hybrid, 82, 95
hydroelectric energy, 23
hydrosphere, 18
hypothesis, 76, 80, 109, 112, 113, 114, 115, 116, 117, 118, 119, 120, 121, 122, 123, 124, 130
igneous rock, 18, 28, 79
immune system, 3, 68
inclined plane, 25
inertia, 24
inferring, 78, 99
infrared light, 23
invertebrates, 27, 133

J
Jupiter, 53, 71, 104

K
kinetic energy, 22, 29, 77
kingdom, Animal, Fungus, Moneran, Plant, Protist, 3

L
laboratory report, 130
Law of the Conservation of Mass, 21
Laws of Motion, 24
lens, 138
lever, 25, 142
life cycles, 9, 44, 67, 84
light energy, 22, 23, 56, 91, 136
liquid, 20, 21, 60, 128, 129
liter, 77
lithosphere, 18
lubricant, 24
Lugol's solution, 135

M
magnet, 24, 57, 75
magnetism, 24, 75
mammals, 27, 50, 68
marble, 28
Mars, 53, 60, 104
mass, 20, 25, 72, 92, 140